How to Opt-Out
of the Technocratic State
By Derrick Broze

Inspired by the work of
Samuel E. Konkin III

Introduction

As humanity enters the second decade of the 21st century, we find ourselves at the precipice of a Technocratic Age where Artificial Intelligence (AI), Smart Technology, and the Internet of Things are becoming a part of everyday life. This technology provides benefits but comes at a cost—corporations, governments, law enforcement, and hackers are all capable of peering into our lives at any moment. Corporations and governments are even learning to use technology in a way that allows them to be the "social engineers" of society. The concept of social credit is also becoming increasingly popular, and the likelihood that citizens will face negative consequences for choosing to speak about controversial topics or criticizing authorities is only going to increase.

This shift toward a world where digital technology is the solution for all things is being driven by the tech sector—specifically the institutions often referred to as Big Wireless and Big Tech. The CEOs of transnational corporations and their partners in government have worked to cement digital technology into every aspect of humanity. The world they envision is one where scientists and technologists are the elite class who decide the future of society. While the digital technology of these industries has only emerged in the last few decades, the philosophy which guides many of the leading figures in industry and government is nearly a century old.

This philosophy of a rule by technological experts and scientists is known as Technocracy. As we will see in the coming chapters, the ideas which underpin this school of thought have quietly been influencing world leaders for decades. *Is this obscure political theory from the 20th century the guiding force behind the move towards a digital dystopia? What are the implications for a world that is always plugged in and on "the grid"? How can one maintain privacy and liberty in a society that is based on mass surveillance, technological control, and the loss of individuality?*

I believe the answers to these questions lie in the writings of political philosopher Samuel Edward Konkin III. Konkin was an activist during the 1960s when talk of revolution in America was at its peak. He believed that using violence to overthrow the State would only result in another leader stepping in and continuing the charade. Konkin also rejected voting, seeing it as participating in an immoral system as well as an inadequate strategy for achieving lasting change. Rather than voting or violence, Konkin proposed a third path for the freedom seeker which he termed Counter-Economics, and more specifically, Agorism. We will explore his work in detail in the coming chapters.

Whether Konkin's vision of freeing the people from the chains of the State becomes reality completely depends on the consciousness of the people. After enough people have been educated about the dangers of the Technocratic Era, there must also be an understanding of the power of non-compliance. If a mass of people find ways to avoid the digital corporate-state we can leverage our numbers and the power of the counter-economy. We can create more freedom and opportunity to live the lives of abundance we desire.

The window is short, but we have the opportunity to remove ourselves from the State's matrix of control. The current social credit system employed in China will soon make its way to the United States and the rest of the "civilized world." It has already become nearly impossible to live a life that is not monitored and analyzed from cradle to grave. If we plan to survive this quickly approaching technocratic corporate-state control grid, I believe we must embrace the solutions first identified by Samuel E. Konkin III. It's time to recognize that Agorism and Counter-Economics are the answer to our problems.

One final note: As I type these words in December 2019, I do so with the full awareness that digital technology is evolving at an exponential rate. The invasive technology of today might appear quaint or even archaic to someone reading this in 2025. I will admit that even the solutions contained within this book may end up outdated in less than a decade depending on the direction our technological world takes. However, no matter what the future looks like **my message to you is never surrender**. Find ways to adapt. Build communities with other like-minded people. Keep the flames of liberty alive in your heart and minds. As long as the human spirit desires to be free, we can and will find a way to overcome all hardship. No matter what year you discover this book, please use it as inspiration and a foundation upon which to build. **Humanity's future in in your hands.**

- Derrick Broze, January 2020

6

Part 1:
Technocracy, Counter-Economics, and the Future of Freedom

The following chapters offer a brief introduction to several concepts including Technocracy, Counter-Economics, and Agorism. In the interest of getting to the "how to" aspect of this presentation we are only going to give an overview of these ideas. For those who want to understand the larger implications of the technocratic movement I recommend author Patrick Wood. If you are interested in a more robust understanding of Counter-Economics and Agorism, I recommend my own book *Manifesto of The Free Humans*, as well as Samuel Konkin's books. I also highly recommend reading Konkin's final unfinished book *Counter-Economics* which is included in Part 3 of this work.

1. What is a Technocracy?

In the early 20th century, a movement began to develop around a political theory known as Technocracy, a system where management of governments is handled by technical experts, often involving technology-focused solutions. The proponents of Technocracy claimed the concept would lead to better management of resources and protection of the planet. However, this system of governance by technological experts and their technology would also involve a loss of privacy, centralization, and management of all human behavior. Although the term appears to have been largely forgotten, the technocratic philosophy and influence can be seen everywhere in our modern digital world.

One of the most influential proponents of Technocracy was a man named Howard Scott, a writer who founded the Technical Alliance in New York City in 1919. Scott believed business owners lacked the necessary skills and data to reform their industries and thus control should be handed over to engineers. In 1932, Scott and fellow technocrat Walter Rautenstrauch formed the "Committee on Technocracy" at Columbia University. The group would eventually splinter, with Scott leading Technocracy Incorporated and technocrat Harold Loeb in charge of the Continental Committee on Technocracy.

In 1938, Technocracy Incorporated released a publication which outlined their vision for a Technocracy (emphasis mine):

*"**Technocracy is the science of social engineering, the scientific operation of the entire social mechanism to produce and distribute goods and services to the entire population of this continent.** For the first time in human history it will be done as a scientific, technical, engineering problem. There will be no place for Politics or Politicians, Finance or Financiers, Rackets or Racketeers. Technocracy states that this method of operating the social mechanism of the North American Continent is now mandatory because we have passed from a state of actual scarcity into the present status of potential abundance in which we are now held to an artificial scarcity forced upon us in order to continue a Price System which can distribute goods only by means of a medium of exchange.*

Technocracy states that price and abundance are incompatible; the greater the abundance the smaller the price. In a real abundance there can be no price at all. **Only by abandoning the interfering price control and substituting a scientific method of production and distribution can an abundance be achieved. Technocracy will distribute by means of a certificate of distribution available to every citizen from birth to death.** *The Technate will encompass the entire American Continent from Panama to the North Pole because the natural resources and the natural boundary of this area make it an independent, self-sustaining geographical unit."*

Technocrats publicized their vision of a centrally planned world with books, speeches, clubs, and political parties. This resulted in a brief period of popularity in the U.S. and Canada in the years following the Great Depression of 1929. As politicians and economists searched for a solution to the financial calamity, the technocrats imagined a world where politicians and business owners were replaced with scientists, engineers, and other technical experts to manage the economy.

However, in the 1940s mainstream interest in the Technocracy movement seemed to dissipate. Some researchers attribute this to a lack of a coherent political theory for achieving change, while others say President Roosevelt and the New Deal provided an alternative solution to financial hardship. Regardless, Technocracy ceased to be a topic of mainstream political discourse even as the industrial revolution spurred on new technologies and previously unseen wealth for those in control of said technology.

The ideas that underpinned the technocratic vision received a notable endorsement in 1970 when political scientist Zbigniew Brzezinski released his book *Between Two Ages: America's Role in the Technetronic Era.* Brzezinski will be familiar to long time researchers of the ruling elite. Until his death in 2018, Brzezinski was a diplomat who ran in the same circles as former Secretary of State and accused war criminal Henry Kissinger and David Rockefeller. Brzezinski served as advisor to several presidents—from Jimmy Carter to Barack

Obama. Brzezinski was also a member of the Atlantic Council, the National Endowment for Democracy, and the Council on Foreign Relations.

Brzezinski's *Between Two Ages* may have changed the term from "Technocracy" to "Technetronic," but the depiction of the future is the same: a world in which the scientific and technological elite centrally plan the lives of all humanity. Essentially, a technologically advanced authoritarian-collectivism where individual liberties are subordinate to the apparent needs of the collective. Brezinski explains Technetronic in the following way:

"The post-industrial society is becoming a "technetronic" society: a society that is shaped culturally, psychologically, socially, and economically by the impact of technology and electronics—particularly in the area of computers and communications. The industrial process is no longer the principal determinant of social change, altering the mores, the social structure, and the values of society...

*In the Technetronic society scientific and technical knowledge, in addition to enhancing production capabilities, quickly spills over to affect almost all aspects of life directly. Accordingly, both the growing capacity for the instant calculation of the most complex interactions and **the increasing availability of biochemical means of human control augment the potential scope of consciously chosen direction, and thereby also the pressures to direct, to choose, and to change.***"

Here are a few more choice quotes from *Between Two Ages: America's Role in the Technetronic Era* which make it clear that the goal is to build a global Technocracy:

"Another threat, less overt but no less basic, confronts liberal democracy. More directly linked to the impact of technology, it involves the gradual appearance of a more controlled and directed society. Such a society would be dominated by an elite whose claim to political power would rest on allegedly superior scientific knowhow. Unhindered by the restraints of traditional liberal values, this elite

10

would not hesitate to achieve its political ends by using the latest modern techniques for influencing public behavior and keeping society under close surveillance and control. Under such circumstances, the scientific and technological momentum of the country would not be reversed but would actually feed on the situation it exploits."

"Persisting social crisis, the emergence of a charismatic personality, and the exploitation of mass media to obtain public confidence would be the steppingstones in the piecemeal transformation of the United States into a highly controlled society."

"Today we are witnessing the emergence of transnational elites, but now they are composed of international businessmen, scholars and public officials. The ties of these new elites cut across national boundaries, their perspectives are not confined by national traditions, and their interests are more functional than national. Increasingly, intellectual elites tend to think in terms of global problems: the need to overcome backwardness, to eliminate poverty, prevent overpopulation, to develop effective peace-keeping machinery. The concern with ideology is yielding to preoccupation with ecology, pollution, overpopulation and the control of disease, drugs, and weather. There is a widespread consensus that functional planning is desirable and that it is the only way to cope with various ecological threats."

"The fiction of sovereignty is clearly no longer compatible with reality. The time has come for a common effort to shape a new framework for international politics. There is already widespread agreement on developing international peace-keeping forces. Emerging global consciousness is forcing the abandonment of preoccupations with national supremacy and accentuating global interdependence."

Brzezinski's vision of the future was not mere speculation or guesswork. He was a member of the ruling class who spent his life using nation states—and the people within them—as pawns in a chess game in which most of the players are dangerously oblivious to the reality unfolding around them. I believe Brzezinski's book describes the world that is unfolding in the early 2020s. I highly recommend diving deep into his work for other fascinating insights into where we are and where we might be headed.

Now that we understand a bit of history of Technocracy and some of the ideas that it proposed we need to examine the world of today to note the Technocratic (or Technetronic if you prefer) influence.

Let's start by looking at the most wealthy companies and most influential CEOs. These individuals are running companies which have amassed large amounts of financial wealth as well as unfathomable amounts of digital data on all of their customers. From Jeff Bezos at Amazon, Bill Gates of Microsoft, Mark Zuckerberg at Facebook, Elon Musk of Tesla, and lesser known names at Google, Apple, and others, these are the technocrats of the early 2020s. Interestingly enough, Musk appears to be walking a path similar to his grandfather, Joshua Haldeman, who was a research director for the Technocracy Incorporated of Canada and national chairman of the Social Credit Party.

These men and their colleagues in various technological industries wield immense power through their companies, wealth, and cultural influence. These individuals have enough money, resources, and connections to shape elections, geoengineer the climate, and cause dips in the stock market, to name a few examples. They are the technocrat class of today.

I want to remind the potential reader of the future that these names might not mean anything to you at this point—they may indeed be relics of a long dead past. Whatever the names of the corporations, CEOs, and governments filling this role the concerns and possible solutions remain the same. If technology continues to advance exponentially, then it is likely that the trend towards surveillance will also continue and with the decrease in privacy, a decrease in overall liberties. This is what we seek to overcome.

12

Another example of the Technocratic world involves the growing use of surveillance tools like facial recognition, voice detection, 24-7 closed-circuit TV cameras, Artificial Intelligence, algorithmic manipulation, cell phone surveillance, social media monitoring, location tracking, digital eavesdropping via smart devices, and the overall push towards a Smart Grid powered by 5G. Of course, these technologies are not promoted as surveillance tools but rather tools for safety, convenience, education, and profit. However, the result is the same: individuals and companies promoting technological solutions to the world's ills, resulting in a loss of individual freedoms and more centralized control.

Of course, selling society on the need for a completely interconnected digital world where technologists and scientific experts organize our lives can be helped along with a healthy dose of propaganda from the State's favorite partner in crime, the corporate media. Brzezinski's *Between Two Ages* provides more insight into the Technocratic plan:

*"In the Technetronic society the trend seems to be toward **aggregating the individual support of millions of unorganized citizens, who are easily within the reach of magnetic and attractive personalities, and effectively exploiting the latest communication techniques to manipulate emotion and control reason.**"*

Together the technocrats (aka Big Tech), their obedient friends in media, and their partners in government are becoming what I call the Technocratic State. The rest of this work is dedicated to poking holes in this Technocratic State and exploiting its weaknesses. As mentioned in the introduction, **those who want to maintain privacy and liberty must be willing to adapt to constantly emerging technologies with the potential to liberate or imprison our hearts and minds.** I believe the key to resisting the Technocracy can be found in the work of Samuel Konkin III and his theory of Counter-Economics.

2. Counter-Economics and Agorism

Note: *Before we get to the "how to" of living a life outside the confines of the increasingly omniscient Technocratic State, we must understand the history and philosophy of Counter-Economics. This chapter includes a run down of the counter-economic strategy, including various definitions offered by Samuel Konkin III. The third chapter further breaks down the philosophy of Agorism. Both chapters were originally published in my third book, Manifesto of the Free Humans, but have been updated to better reflect the specific nature of this book. I include them here as a brief introduction to the concepts of Counter-Economics and Agorism.*

It is my hope that this distillation of Samuel Konkin's work will help readers understand that these strategies can be employed in your life—regardless of age, race, religion, ethnicity, gender, political affiliation, socioeconomic status, or any other division of the human species. Quite simply, Counter-Economics is a strategy that can be practiced by anyone anywhere in the world. For readers who are new to this field of research, I recommend checking out Konkin's New Libertarian Manifesto and An Agorist Primer. For those who are familiar with Counter-Economics and Agorism, I recommend skipping ahead to Chapter 4.

In 1979, anarchist, activist, and writer Samuel E. Konkin III (SEK3) released *The New Libertarian Manifesto*, presenting his case for a strain of libertarianism that he called "New Libertarianism." The philosophy behind the New Libertarian Movement was Agorism, named after the "agora," the Greek word for marketplace. We will elaborate on Agorism in a moment, but essentially it is a radical philosophy that seeks to create a society free of coercion and force by encouraging people to opt-out of the corporate-state control grid. Konkin believed if a movement of people pulled their money, time, and support from corporate and state power, it would siphon away enough resources to collapse the State. As the State collapsed the agorists would help build systems that are not based on violence and coercion.

Konkin called on individuals to exit the mainstream economic system because he was one of the first modern thinkers to recognize that the unregulated market is the largest market in the world. Sometimes known as system-d, alternative, or informal economy, the value of this untaxed and unregulated market has a market value in the trillions of dollars. Throughout history, when a government or king has tried to enforce prohibition—be that drugs, alcohol, gambling, sex, or books—they inadvertently cause a growth in the underground economy or, as Konkin called it, the counter-economy. Upon recognizing that the State has been incapable to slow the growth of the counter-economy Konkin saw an opportunity to disempower the State and preserve liberty for the people.

Konkin termed this strategy "Counter-Economics," which he defined as the *"theory and practice of all human action neither accepted by the State nor involving any initiatory violence or threat of violence."* Throughout the years, Konkin continuously refined his understanding and writing on the topic, and in doing so he offered several definitions and background on Counter-Economics:

"An explanation of how people keep their wealth and property from the State is then Counter-Establishment economics, or Counter- Economics for short. The actual practice of human actions that evade, avoid and defy the State is countereconomic activity, but in the same sloppy way "economics" refers to both the science and what it studies, Counter- Economics will undoubtedly be used. Since this writing is Counter-Economic theory itself, what will be referred to as Counter-Economics is the practice." (The New Libertarian Manifesto)

"A Counter-Economist is (1) anyone practicing a counter-economic act; (2) one who studies such acts. Counter-Economics is the (1) practice (2) study of counter-economic acts."
(*An Agorist Primer*)

"Counter-Economics is doing what you want, when you want, for your own good reasons." (Counter-Economics)

"Counter-Economics sounds like counter-culture; indeed, the term was chosen with that in mind. Where the Counterculture rejected an Establishment "culture"

and its values in the 1960s, the counter-economists reject the Establishment economics as just as corrupt. Much of the counterculture was counter-economic, much of it was not. **Anti-economics is not Counter-Economics; in fact, Counter-Economics as theory was developed from what could be called an orthodox revolt against an heretical, impure, Establishment economics."**
(Counter-Economics)

I have always seen Counter-Economics as a method of aligning your actions with your stated goals and principles. If you don't support illegal wars of aggression, then find ways to avoid paying taxes or donate your taxes to a charity (see: War Tax Resistance). If you're tired of central banks manipulating the State's currency and enslaving you via funny money, then avoid the State's money, use alternative currency, barter, reduce your need for money, etc.

Counter-Economics suggests that moral people break bad laws by choosing to consciously opt out of systems that do not align with their values. As Konkin wrote in the unfinished *Counter-Economics*:

"Countereconomic activity is any human action that takes place without the approval of the State. And since laws cover almost every human endeavor, often prohibiting both the action and its corresponding inaction, **everyone to at least some small degree must bend or break laws simply to exist."**

Being a counter-economist means that when you run into a roadblock to your liberty and health you find a way around it. This can include using or creating alternative currencies, community gardening efforts which provide an opportunity to be free of big corporate grocery stores, tax resistance, operating a business without licenses so your hard-earned money doesn't go to the State, and more. Counter-Economics also extends to the creation of alternative education programs, free schools or skill shares, and independent media ventures that counter the establishment narratives.

The reality is that the counter-economy is all around you. Every time someone pays a neighbor in cash to mow the lawn or do handiwork, they are participating in the counter-economy. The transaction does not involve taxes going to the State and the cash makes it a non-digital, untraceable transaction. If you have ever shopped at a garage sale, flea market, or pop up shop and not paid taxes—or perhaps even paid with an alternative currency—you have been a counter-economist. Of course, most of the public who participate in the counter/underground/alternative economy do not realize the potential and likely have never heard of Konkin or Counter-Economics. He believed a raising in the consciousness and awareness of the power of the counter-economy could create a mass movement of people exiting the system and building new ways outside of the Technocratic State.

For a deeper understanding of Konkin's work let's take a look at his writing on Agorism. It is important to note that one need not self-identify as a new libertarian, libertarian, agorist, or anarchist to appreciate and make use of Counter-Economics. Simply put, one can practice Counter-Economics for the benefits it offers in escaping the Technocracy while not completely agreeing with Konkin's theories. However, I share this research because I believe his ideas offer a viable path forward.

Understanding Agorism

In the *New Libertarian Manifesto*, SEK3 outlines his vision for a more free and just world by first describing society's present condition: Statism. Statism is the tendency for citizens of a nation to view the State as the mechanism for which change can be brought about. Thus, a statist is someone who blindly trusts in the authority of the State and always reaches to the State as the solution to society's ills.

Konkin briefly outlines the path of human thinking, from slavery to the discovery of libertarian thought, and emphasizes the importance of consistency between means and ends. Indeed, Konkin believes that exposing Statist inconsistencies is *"the most crucial activity of the libertarian theorist."* From here, Konkin describes the goal of Agorism and the counter-economic means necessary to achieve this goal.

In order to paint a clear picture of the agorist struggle for a more free world, Konkin explains the four stages from Statism to Agorism as well as various actions that a consciously practicing agorist might seize upon in order to advance agorist propaganda and counter-economic activity. By understanding Konkin's vision of progress it is possible to create a diagram to outline how far society as a whole has come and where we, as individuals, fit within these steps. After the steps have been mapped it will be possible to pinpoint strategies that can help the new libertarian move from one stage to the next.

Konkin begins in "Phase Zero: Zero-Density Agorist Society." Phase Zero is the time when agorists did not exist and libertarian thought was scattered and unorganized, which Konkin says has been *"most of human history."* Once libertarians became aware of the philosophy of Agorism, counter-economic activity began and we moved into "Phase 1: Low-Density Agorist Society."

In this phase, the first counter-economic libertarians appear. Konkin believed that this was a dangerous time for activists who would be tempted by "Get-Liberty-Quick" schemes. Konkin also reminds agorists not to be tempted by political campaigns. *"All will fail if for no other reason than Liberty grows individual by individual. Mass conversion is impossible,"* he wrote.

Phase 1 is presented at a time where the main goal of the few practicing counter-economists is recruitment and creation of "radical caucuses"—or what I call *Freedom Cells.* Konkin also notes that the majority of society is acting *"with little understanding of any theory but who are induced by material gain to evade, avoid, or defy the State. Surely they are a hopeful potential?"*

In order to achieve the free society Konkin again emphasizes the need for education and *"consciousness-raising of counter-economists to libertarian understanding and mutual supportiveness."* SEK3 also called for the creation of a movement which may grow strong enough in influence and numbers in the latter stages of Phase 1 to be able to *"block marginal actions by the State."* The ability to block actions by the State has absolutely increased in recent years with the explosion of decentralized, peer-to-peer networks via the Internet that allow for rapid sharing of information and calls to organize. There is a growing number of videos on the Internet showing communities banding together to oppose unjust arrests by agents of the State.

For example, the websites and apps FreedomCells.org, NextDoor.com, and GetCell411.com offer tools that can be used to strengthen our communities, grow the counter-economy, and push back against the State. By using the Freedom Cell Network, one can locate other freedom-minded individuals within their city, state, or country with the specific goal of organizing in the real world and bypassing the need for government.

In 2016, we launched FreedomCells.org as an online platform for building mutual aid groups known as Freedom Cells which we will explore in detail in the next chapter. NextDoor also allows the user to connect with the local community, both digitally and in the real world. The app has the added benefit of being focused on a specific neighborhood. This allows individuals to post important safety information, lost and found items, or counter-economic business opportunities directly to those who live near them. Finally, Cell411 describes itself as a *"real time, free emergency management platform."* This means it allows you to create "cells" or groups to which you can send out direct alerts in the case of a flat tire, car accident, violence from an agent of the State, or some other emergency. The app also allows for truly agorist ridesharing where a third party does not dictate the price of the trip or the currency that must be used.

Note: *Once again, to the potential reader of the future, if these apps and websites have been made irrelevant due to time and technological advances, it is important to ensure we as free people have alternatives to the State and corporations.*

Each of these tools are a part of the technology of the counter-economy which have the potential to render government intervention and regulation completely useless. If we seize the moment we can grow the black and grey markets using these emerging peer-to-peer platforms. This is exactly what Konkin believed would help society progress from Phase 1 to Phase 2.

As we move to "Phase 2: Mid-Density, Small Condensation Agorist Society," the statists take notice of Agorism. Is it in this phase that Konkin believes the counter-economy will grow and agorists will begin to represent *"an ever-larger agorist sub-society embedded in the statist society."* Although the majority of agorists are still living within the State's claimed territories we begin to see a *"spectrum of the degree of agorism in most individuals."* This includes benefactors of the State who are *"highly statist"* and *"a few fully conscious of the agorist alternative,"* however the majority of society is still engaged in the Statist Economy.

From here, Konkin suggests that agorists may want to start condensing into districts, ghettos, islands, or space colonies. We are in fact beginning to see the creation of agorist minded communities, seasteaders, eco-villages, co-ops, and underground spaces which emphasize counter-economic activity and the creation of counter-institutions to the State. Konkin believed these agorist communities might be able to count on the sympathy of mainstream society to prevent an attack from the State.

This is the moment where the question of community protection and defense comes into play. We have seen the creation of community protection alternatives to the police state monopoly (see the Threat Management Center in Detroit and the Autodefensas in Mexico), but thus far nothing completely agorist has come into existence. It is the creation of these syndicates of community protection which will ultimately allow the agora to flourish. However, for this to happen *"the entire society has been contaminated by agorism to a degree,"* leading to the possible creation of an above or underground movement which Konkin called the New Libertarian Alliance (NLA). The NLA simply acts as the spokesperson for the agora and uses *"every chance to publicize the superiority of agorist living to statist inhabiting and perhaps argue for tolerance of those with 'different ways'."*

This brings us to "Phase 3: High-Density, Large Condensation, Agorist Society," which is described as the point when the State has moved into a terminal crisis period due in part to *"the sapping of the State's resources and corrosion of its authority by the growth of the Counter-Economy."* As the agora grows in influence the State's stranglehold also dissipates because of unsustainable economic practices. Konkin again warns that the statists will attempt to win over new libertarians with *"anti-principles"* and calls for maintaining *"vigilance and purity of thought."* Highly motivated new libertarians move into R&D to help create the first agorist protection and arbitration agencies that will compete with the State. At this point, government exists in pockets with the State mostly concentrated in one geographic territory. Those living under statism are very aware of the freedom being experienced by their agorist counterparts. The State has become weak enough that *"large syndicates of market protection agencies"*

20

can contain the State and defend new libertarians who sign up for protection-insurance. This, Konkin believed, was *"the final step before the achievement of a libertarian society."* Society is divided between the larger agorist areas and the isolated statist centers.

The transition from Phase 3 to Phase 4 brings about *"the last unleashing of violence by the ruling class of the state."* Konkin said that once the State's intellectuals recognize that their authority is no longer respected, they will choose to attack. Defense against the State will be managed after the counter-economy has generated the syndicates of protection agencies large enough to defend against the remaining statists. The NLA should work to prevent the State from recognizing its weaknesses until the agorist movement has completely infected the statist society. Once the agorist communities have successfully resisted the State's attack, the agorist revolution will be complete. As we move from Phase 3 to 4, Konkin notes that the first three changes *"are actually rather artificial divisions; no abrupt change occurs from first to second to third."* However, he envisions the change from the third to the fourth phases to be "quite sudden."

In Phase 4, "Agorist Society with Statist Impurities", the State has gasped its dying breath and the counter-economy becomes the freed market where exchanges are free of coercion. Konkin predicts that *"division of labor and self-respect of each worker-capitalist-entrepreneur will probably eliminate the traditional business organization—especially the corporate hierarchy, an imitation of the State and not the Market."* He imagines companies as associations of independent contractors, consultants, and entrepreneurs. After the remnants of the State are apprehended and brought to justice, freedom becomes the basis of ordinary life and *"we tackle the other problems facing mankind."*

Whether the totality of Konkin's vision becomes realized, the world has at the very least made some slight progress through the phases predicted in the *New Libertarian Manifesto*. All signs point to the counter-economy and consciously practicing agorist movement to be somewhere at the tail end of Phase 1 and merging into Phase 2. As mentioned above, the Internet (and technology as a whole) has greatly increased the chances for success of the Konkian revolution. While humanity is being exposed to the value of a life free of coercion, they have not yet been properly exposed to the tools with which to create such a world. If the agorist movement and counter-economy continue to expand in equal rates to the violence and theft of the State, it will only be a matter of time before we see protection agencies with the capacity to defend the people. Konkin believed that once the people recognize the State is weakened and in decline, they will naturally gravitate towards the counter-economy, leading his agorist vision to become reality.

Clearly the people of the world have a desire to exchange their goods and services without oppressive, elitist barriers to entry in the marketplace. The people desire to voluntarily associate and exchange without interference or intervention. This desire will *always* lead to the creation of counter-economic activity in the black and grey markets as long as the "mainstream" statist economy is subject to the whims of the current puppets in control. However, seeking to escape the State's regulation is not the only goal to our agorist and counter-economic strategy. **The endgame is a stateless society where free people are not bound by the force and coercion of the parasitic state and corporate class.**

Though it is rarely discussed in public schools or the mainstream media, there are several examples of stateless societies and communities existing throughout history. For those interested in studying past stateless societies, I recommend studying James Scott's *The Art of Not Being Governed: An Anarchist History of Upland Southeast Asia*; *A Century of Anarchy: Neutral Moresnet Through the Revisionist Lens*; and Pierre Clastres' *Society Against the State*.

3. Vertical and Horizontal Agorism

"As more people reject the State's mystifications—nationalism, pseudo-Economics, false threats, and betrayed political promises—the Counter-Economy grows both vertically and horizontally. Horizontally, it involves more and more people who turn more and more of their activities toward the counter-economic; vertically, it means new structures (businesses and services) grow specifically to serve the Counter- Economy (safe communication links, arbitrators, insurance for specifically "illegal" activities, early forms of protection technology, and even guards and protectors). Eventually, the "underground" breaks into the overground where most people are agorists, few are statists, and the nearest State enforcement cannot effectively crush them."

- SEK III, Applied Agorism, *An Agorist Primer*

We are going to take a look at two different types of counter-economic action that are applicable to a variety of individuals in a range of living situations. I refer to these strategies as Vertical and Horizontal Agorism. We are working with two complementary definitions of horizontal and vertical that further explain the "how to" of agorist philosophy. These definitions are taken from the above quote from Samuel Konkin III and from Swedish Austrian economist Per Bylund and his 2006 essay *A Strategy for Forcing the State Back*. Let's compare the definitions and see how they can provide a path for the curious counter-economist.

Konkin starts by describing the counter-economy as growing horizontally in the sense of an increasing portion of the mainstream population turning their activities towards the non-statist economy. Vertical growth, in the Konkian sense, involves the actual creation of counter-institutions to the statist counterparts. This means building alternatives not only to the economic power centers via alternative currencies but alternatives to the deadstream corporate media, the corporate food production systems, the compliant academic centers, and the growing non-profit industrial complex.

Per Bylund describes his vision of vertical Agorism as the "introvert" strategy based on the work and ideas of radical libertarian Karl Hess. Hess was an extremely eloquent speaker and speechwriter who grew from conservative to libertarian anarchist to a more left-leaning community organizer and activist. During the 1960s, he was heavily involved in organizing on campus during the rise of the new left and anti-war student movements. Hess worked with Murray Rothbard, Konkin, Carl Ogelsby of the Students for a Democratic Society, and several others in an attempt to forge alliances between the emerging new left and libertarian movements. He was also one of the few people to have 100 percent of his wages stolen by the IRS for challenging the income tax.

In the 1970s, Hess shifted the focus of his activism to experiment in community building within the low income neighborhood of Adams-Morgan in Washington D.C. In his books *Community Technology* and *Neighborhood Power* Hess outlines how he worked with the local neighborhood to build an empowered community focused on sustainability—or what they termed "appropriate technology." Hess describes a neighborhood with aquaponic gardening in basements, rooftop gardens, and community services meant to replace the State options. He was adamant that tools and technology directly contribute to freedom. By being able to share tools with your community members you can share access to the means of production and encourage entrepreneurship.

It is this focus on community empowerment that Per Bylund refers to as the vertical or introvert strategy. These actions can be considered agorist in the sense that they are aimed at building self and community reliance rather than dependence on external forces, but they are not explicitly counter-economic because they do not involve black and grey markets. Still, these vertical actions are extremely valuable and necessary.

Vertical Agorism includes participating in and creating community exchange networks, urban farming, backyard gardening, farmers markets, supporting alternatives to the police, and supporting peer-to-peer decentralized technologies. While these vertical steps could potentially involve the use of the State's currency (and therefore not completely counter-economic), they are still significant for challenging the dependency on the State and corporate classes

24

Other vertical steps may not directly involve exchanging currency but still work against dependency. This could include both moral support and promotion of technologies that disrupt the status quo and foster stronger relationships among community members.

One very pronounced example of vertical Agorism is seen in the growing alternative media which has been made possible by the Internet. Less than one generation ago, the mainstream media, owned by mega-corporations and tightly regulated by government, controlled all of the information that filtered down to society. The distribution of information in society came from the top down making it very easy to brainwash and propagandize the population. However, with the rise of the Internet activists and freedom-seeking individuals discovered they could use this new medium to create their own media, become journalists themselves, and fight back against the propaganda of the State. In just a few short years, the alternative media quickly upset the monopoly of the mainstream media, taking up large portions of their once exclusive market share. The surge of independent media provides an excellent example in our study of how alternative systems and institutions can be created to compete with existing State monopolies. (Unfortunately, the Corporate-State nexus has permeated social media as well and censorship of independent voices is now pervasive as of 2019.)

The goal is to question and challenge the mechanisms of power that seek to influence and rule over our lives. This includes the State as well as other institutions that attempt to exert control and influence. For example, by choosing to grow your own food or support local farmers, you are taking a vertical step away from the biotechnology corporations that promote the heavy use of pesticides and a potentially hazardous technology. You are also not supporting the transportation of food products from thousands of miles away. Instead, you walk to your backyard or the local market for your produce. This greatly increases your independence while terminating support for an unsustainable industry. These vertical steps are also the easiest ways to begin living in line with your principles. Once again, we can see the value of consistency of words and actions.

Per Bylund describes the horizontal, or extrovert strategy, as more directly related to Konkin's ideas. The extrovert label is related to the bold choice to pursue actions the State considers to be illegal or immoral. By venturing into this territory you are joining the ranks of the bootlegger, the moonshiner, the cannabis dealer, the guerrilla gardener, the weapons dealer, the crypto-anarchist, and the unlicensed lawn mower, food vendor, or barber. When one combines the vertical and horizontal agorist strategy an image comes into view that illustrates the steps a wide range of people can take in a variety of living situations and environments.

In the bottom left corner we have Statism and in the top right corner we have Agorism. We can plot vertical actions that help lift the individual up from dependency. Perhaps your situation is better suited to vertical actions such as growing your own food, using encrypted messaging, hosting community skill shares at your house, practicing peaceful parenting tactics, providing alternatives to State welfare by crowdfunding money for community projects and feeding the homeless, or simply cleaning up the neighborhood. Each of these steps moves the individual (and in the long-term, the community) vertically towards consistency and independence. For those who are ready to become counter-economists and take on the risks of grey and black market activity we plot their actions both vertically and horizontally. An agorist practicing horizontally and vertically would move up and away from Statism and dependency to the top right position of Agorism. This means that for every garden built, alternative currency used, tax

26

avoided, skill shared, business practiced without a license, and illegal substance sold the individual can plot their progress moving from dependency to self-reliance and from Statism to Agorism.

When Konkin first espoused the concept of Agorism the consciously practicing counter-economy may have only involved a few radical libertarians. But since that time the opportunities for black and grey market exchanges have grown immensely. As the State's weaknesses become apparent it will become safer for the masses to begin exiting the former economy and joining the counter-economy. This is the truly freed market or agora of which Konkin spoke.

Remember we cannot defeat the Technocratic State by using their technology blindly as this will only serve to empower them. We must create and support alternatives to the State's monopolies whenever and wherever possible. It will take brave counter-economists venturing into uncharted territories, making mistakes, occasionally falling victim to the State's laws, and learning how to better our approach. We need these pioneers to lay the groundwork so that others will not have to face the same difficulties in the future. As these trail blazers light the way. we also expect to see a growth of free communities and freedom networks around the world.

I have a vision of thousands of interlocking autonomous communities comprised of empowered individuals with a variety of unique ideas and expressions of the human experience. These communities are voluntarily trading and sharing skills without the violence inherent to our current paradigm and without the constant invasions of privacy. I believe this world can be achieved with an organized effort to spread agorist philosophy and increase participation in the counter-economy via Vertical and Horizontal Agorism and the concept of Freedom Cells which we will cover in Part 2.

4. The Drawbacks (And Solutions) to
Living the Counter-Economic Lifestyle

The reasons one chooses to opt-out of "traditional" institutions and societal expectations vary from person to person, but generally people are looking to stop supporting systems they do not agree with. Whether we are talking financially (to avoid taxation) or philosophically (on moral grounds), many of us who live outside of the mainstream system do so because we disagree with the people running these systems—and in some cases, the system altogether.

We do not want to fund these governments by complying with taxation. We do not want to support the monopolized banking system and the banks that rob the people. We do not want to violate our moral compass or principles by participating in these charades. Instead, we take steps to begin removing ourselves from these systems as quickly (and safely) as possible. We each have a different goal and different perspectives on how far to push the effort to opt-out and vacate these systems that promote authoritarianism and financial theft. However, what unites us is our belief that **people should be free to organize their own affairs without the interference of centralized authority in the form of government or monarchs.** Put simply, we acknowledge that every individual owns themselves and should be able to live free of interference, extortion, threats of violence, and forced compassion.

When I came to these conclusions, I had an internal shift that was so profound and simple: *I will no longer participate in systems I do not support.* First, I stopped using banks because I saw the results of the 2008 financial crisis and I learned about the many economic crises created by banksters throughout history. Second, I refused to use a credit card and never attempted to establish a credit line through these banks. I also stopped driving because I didn't want to get a State ID and instead only use a passport. By the end of 2010, I came to understand the nature of war and violence being perpetuated by the American Empire and decided I would no longer pay an income tax. I stopped filing and have made efforts to keep my income below the Poverty Line. I also stopped working jobs which compenstated me in the form of a check.

Since that time I have started a couple of businesses of my own (without filing paperwork for city licenses) and only accepted cash, silver, or cryptocurrency. All of my income has been in metals, cash, digital payments, or bartering. Obviously, I am still paying a sales tax when I am not shopping at a farmers market or buying directly from a gray market entrepreneur, but the goal is to take steps towards completely opting-out. It doesn't happen overnight and it doesn't come without struggle. Let's take a moment to look at some of these struggles and their potential solutions.

First, what are the potential downsides to not using a bank? Before we answer that question we should note that there are alternatives to the big banks, including local credit unions and co-ops. These institutions are typically more connected to the local community and not involved in economic theft. However, do your research and use these alternatives at your own risk. One criticism of going bank-free is a fear of lack of security when not storing funds in a traditional banking institution. The fact is, you can put your trust in a banking institution and the U.S. government, or you can choose to take personal responsibility and store your money under the mattress, in a safe, in a private bank, or anywhere else you please so as long as you are taking proper security measures.

Beyond the security risks, there are also financial downsides to not using banks. I recently received payment in the form of a check for a media gig. Not only was I forced to visit a bank to cash the check (Bank of America, no less), but I was taxed $8 by the bank to cash my check for not opening a bank account. Now, this problem is easily remedied by ongoing education about the value of not using banks (or government backed money) and the power of alternative currencies. Unfortunately, we are still at a point where too few people know and understand these values, resulting in limited options in the market. The company that sent me the check is an old media company whose employees are ignorant to agorist philosophy, Counter-Economics, and digital payment options. The likelihood of my convincing them to pay me in silver or crypto is not high. This is important to remember because until we have built a completely parallel system that offers an alternative to the current paradigm – in every area of our lives – we will occasionally have to conduct business with people who are still filing taxes and therefore keep a record of every financial transaction.

Another recent issue I have encountered involves the renting or purchasing of property. In my case, I was attempting to rent an apartment in a big city, but these obstacles apply elsewhere as well. Because I have rented through different people for years, it has become increasingly difficult to do so on my own as I have less and less records to show to potential landlords or Realtors. In the most recent case I found several potential properties, contacted the property owners, and attempted to negotiate my way into a new home. I have no problem paying rent on time, but my lack of check stubs causes issues with individuals looking for traditional forms of payment.

Again, when I attempt to explain that I receive money from supporters via Patreon, money via this crazy thing called cryptocurrency, and some money in cash, they usually look at me with a confused expression on their face. I explain that I can show them payments received via Paypal but that does not seem to satisfy either. From there, property owners tend to ask to see a bank statement. When I say no, they are baffled and then ask for a tax record. When I tell them I don't have that either, they look at me as though I have personally disrespected their mother. By the end of these conversations I am being told they cannot rent to me because I have no way to verify my income.

So what is the solution to these problems? The most obvious solution is education. Those of us who value the idea that all moral people should opt-out of immoral systems and create new ones, ought to spend our time and energy educating others about the value of such actions. The more people who understand this concept, the more entrepreneurs there are opting-out and creating value in the counter-economy. Now as far as the banking situation, cryptocurrencies are showing the world what digital decentralized banking looks like. The more energy we put into supporting (or creating) alternative currencies – digital or otherwise – the less power the centralized banking monopolies have.

As far as solutions for renting an apartment when you live mostly outside of the system, I believe blockchain technology offers hope. Blockchain is the peer-to-peer, digital ledger technology behind Bitcoin and other cryptos. To understand how blockchain can help, we have to think about why Realtors and property owners want to see documentation from a bank or a government. Trust. Security. Due to the massive amount of propaganda promoted in public schooling, most people grow up believing these institutions to be an essential part of life, if not a benevolent force in our lives. We are taught to trust and cooperate with these institutions. The average person does not trust or believe someone is authentic or valuable or rent-worthy if they do not possess such documentation.

So imagine if every week when I am paid for the articles I write, I take a screenshot of the digital payment (or a picture of someone paying me cash for a job well done) and post it on a blockchain. The blockchain is decentralized, meaning posts cannot be altered or deleted. If I continue to post my weekly income statements on a blockchain, I would have a decentralized and transparent record of my history or any other documents I chose to place on the blockchain. In fact, this could already happen by making posts on a website like Steemit. If the Realtor or property owner understands blockchain or is willing to learn, they can feel secure because there is a record of my pay. We could even sign a contract together on the blockchain. This would allow for transparency and security on both sides.

I believe solutions like this are the future and we are starting to see this unfold. For the moment there are difficulties as we agorist pioneers lay the groundwork for the counter-economy and the next stage of human evolution. Do your part to create the future by educating yourself and others about Agorism and Counter-Economics.

(This essay was originally published in the Counter-Markets Newsletter)

Part 2:
Counter-Economics
as a Solution to Technocracy

The following essays are my original writing combined with SEK3's notes for his final unwritten chapters. I chose not to finish all of his unfinished chapters and instead focused on the areas which I feel have the most potential to educate the reader about counter-economics. I am indebted to SEK3 for his notes and inspiration.

5. Counter-Economics In the Digital Age

Up to this point we have shared the history of Technocracy, the strategy of Counter-Economics, and Agorism. We also explored how the counter-economic path has the potential to be the solution to our digital dystopia. Now we will discuss the solutions to living a life as free from the grip of the Technocratic State as possible.

In addition to being an anarchist philosopher, Konkin was also a fan of science fiction. These two interests merged with his "discovery" of Counter-Economics, for it was his appreciation of the sci-fi genre which lead him to propose that technology could play a role in freeing the people from the chains of bondage and expand the counter-economy. Konkin died in 2004, shortly before social media, cryptocurrency, and digital encryption became mainstream. Long before bitcoin or cryptocurrency emerged, Konkin was discussing similar concepts and predicting that new computer technology would facilitate counter-economic activity. However, Konkin was not a fool. He realized that the authorities would use the emerging digital technology to expand state control.

As someone who has spent the last seven years promoting Konkin's ideas, I recognize that the Technocratic State threatens to remove the ability to safely opt out of the corporate-state system. We are in desperate need for solutions to maintain the anonymity and privacy needed to safely navigate the counter-economy under the digital dystopian world we are now living in. It is not clear if Konkin could see the direction in which the world was headed when he left this planet, but I have found myself contemplating this issue. Which brings us to the following conversation.

What does it mean to be a counter-economist in the Age of the Surveillance State? How can one participate in the underground economy when Big Brother is always watching? Will it be possible to starve the State once social credit scores become mandatory?

Let's start by examining the current landscape of the world concerning digital surveillance and overall privacy. As of 2020 the majority of the "developed" world has adopted the use of some type of digital technology including cell phones, tablets, laptops, desktops, or wearable digital tech. The middle class and higher are falling in line with the latest fad of smart everything, surrounding themselves with technology that can listen, record, and/or watch their daily lives. From door bell cameras to home assistants and TVs that are always listening, the masses are voluntarily abandoning privacy in the name of entertainment and convenience.

Simultaneously, law enforcement and government agencies continue to claim they need all manner of high tech gadgets to prevent terrorism and violent crime. Cell phone surveillance tools, license plate cameras, facial recognition cameras, radars that can see through walls, secret surveillance planes, social media monitoring, DNA collection, gait detection, voice detection, and threat scores – these tools are increasingly available to departments willing to pay up. There are also semi-private mega corporations buying up every bit of data they can find on potential consumers. This data is used to sell us things we don't need, monitor our daily habits, and will eventually pressure every individual to be obedient to the Technocratic State under threat of punishment and exclusion from the digital world.

In 2019, consumer tech organization Comparitech found that the United States, China, Malaysia, Pakistan, India, Indonesia, Phillipines, and Taiwan were the worst offenders when it came to protecting the privacy of people's biometric data. Comparitech said that these nations use biometric data to a *"severe and invasive extent."* Indeed, the Technocracy is a growing problem around the world.

In the U.S., the Federal Bureau of Investigations (FBI) has been fighting for years to keep secret a database containing hundreds of millions of "face prints" from American citizens and non-citizens alike. It is important to note that facial recognition technology is not just about scanning someone's face. Newer software is also learning to evaluate (and predict) your emotions and state of mind. The FBI has also been waging a war against encryption, fearing that the people might develop an unbreakable code and thus maintain some level of privacy.

The U.S. Transportation Safety Agency (TSA) has begun testing facial recognition technology at select airports for international travelers with plans to expand the program in 2021 and 2023. The U.S. government has expressed interest in expanding the program to all travelers. The plans for this type of biometric control grid in the U.S. were set into motion by the Illegal Immigration Reform and Immigrant Responsibility Act of 1996 and expanded after the attacks of September 11, 2001. However, there has been some successful push back against the Technocracy. As of December 2019, three different U.S. cities have banned or regulated facial recognition software pending further study.

In November 2019, France became the first European country to use facial recognition technology as part of a nationwide digital identity for citizens. The new government app is operated by using facial recognition and will give users access to around 500 government websites. Those who choose not to participate would theoretically be locked out of accessing these government websites.

Citizens of India are already finding themselves locked out of the Aadhaar biometric ID program. Under this system reports have begun to emerge detailing instances of citizens being refused access to services due to Aadhaar glitches and ultimately dying of starvation as a result. The program launched in 2009 with the goal of giving every single Indian citizens a unique, biometrically verified identification number. By the end of 2019, an estimated 1.2 billion Indians were enrolled in the program. Users have their iris and/or finger prints scanned and then receive a unique 12-digit number linked to their biometric and demographic data. They will then use this identification number when getting married, setting up a bank account, paying taxes, signing up for a cell phone contract, or even when starting a digital wallet. Again, it appears obvious that those who find a way to avoid the system will be locked out of mainstream society.

China is perhaps the best current example of an advanced authoritarian Technocratic State and likely the model for the rest of the world. Another 2019 study from Comparitech reported that eight of the top ten most-surveilled cities in the world can be found in China. By 2022 China is projected to have one public closed-circuit television (CCTV) camera for every two people. The estimated 200 million CCTV cameras are part of a "Skynet" network active across China. The Chinese government has also started collecting citizen's DNA

35

to build a DNA database. The government has come under fire for detention centers built for Uyghurs, a Muslim minority population which has been forced to install a spyware app on their phones and submit to biometric recognition. However, the Chinese government claims that the detention centers are voluntary vocational training centers. In December 2019, the Chinese government implemented a new rule requiring China's 854 million Internet users to use facial identification in order to apply for new Internet or mobile services.

Equally disturbing is the ongoing rollout of the nationwide social credit system. Starting in 2009, the Chinese government began testing a national reputation system based on a citizen's economic and social reputation or "social credit." This social credit score can be used to reward or punish certain behaviors. By late 2019 Chinese citizens were losing points on their score for dishonest and fraudulent financial behavior, playing loud music, eating on public transportation, jaywalking, running red lights, failing to appear at doctor appointments, missing job interviews or hotel reservation without canceling, and incorrectly sorting waste. To raise one's social credit score a Chinese citizen can donate blood, donate to an approved charity, volunteer for community service, and other activities approved by the government. The Chinese government has begun to deny millions of people the ability to purchase plane and high-speed rail tickets due to low social credit scores and being labeled "untrustworthy."

This is the world of the early 21st century. If we assume technology will continue to advance exponentially then it is probably a safe bet that the surveillance and privacy concerns are here to stay. Unless there is some sort of resistance to these dangers privacy will be completely eroded within a decade. For the moment these technologies are mostly voluntary. For example you don't have to buy the latest digital home assistant device and you don't have to carry a cell phone with you everywhere you go. This means you have the power to decide what type of products and companies you support with your purchases and how you interact with technology. We don't have to blindly submit and opt-in to every latest tech update or advancement.

The more immediate and threatening element of the Technocracy is the State. While corporations are gathering massive amounts of data from individuals who have chosen to purchase or use certain products, the government is able to leverage their perceived legitimate authority to force the populations to submit to biometric technology. History is rife with examples of masses of people being propagandized to work against their own interests. While the collective population may be easily swayed, there will always be individuals who hold out.

We as individuals can choose to opt out of mandatory biometrics and social credit schemes. But if everyone around us is still opting-in it is likely they will choose not to associate with those who have a low social credit scores. Some people will do this out of fear that their own score will decrease for hanging out with "untrustworthy" types. I can hear it now: *"You know I love you, man, but if my score drops any lower I won't be able to take the family out of the country for vacation."* Or *"I won't be able to get that loan, buy that car, or visit public parks"*–the list goes on. **This is the real power of social engineering.**

As we outlined above the Technocratic State is growing around the world. This means at some point in the near future YOU will have to make a choice. *Will you submit to mandatory facial recognition in order to travel? Will you submit to biometrics in exchange for continued access to government services? What will you do when the 5G Smart Grid is everywhere from big city to countryside? Will you give your car insurance company access to your location for a discounted rate? Are you already using your fingerprints or your face to unlock your cell phone or your home?*

The answer to these questions will determine your future. I am operating under the assumption that if you found your way to this book you are at the very least curious about what it takes to live a thriving life that is not under the thumb of the Technocratic State. If that is your goal then you have a few options:

1. Hold Down the Fort - This option is for the person that has no interest or ability to leave home for some other (potentially better) option. If you are committed to your home or have no other option then this would be you. You can either waste away and march with the rest of the sheep to the slaughter or you can try to create change. Find ways to reach others and educate them about the dangers. This might involve fighting for political change on the local level, passing out flyers, phone banking, or social media campaigns. I understand we cannot all be full-time activists, but each of us can find a way to contribute to the goal of creating a community of people who voluntarily choose to opt-out of the Technocratic State. Of course, the closer you are to a big city and "civilization" the harder it will be to avoid the growing Technocracy.

2. Exit and Build - This involves leaving your base of operations behind and moving to a location with less invasive practices and less technocratic corporate-state influence. If you have decided you are living in an area that has no hope and would rather start fresh then you should exit and build something that reflects your values. This could be done solo, as a couple, with family, and even with friends. Perhaps you purchase land, share living space, or live adjacent to each other in a neighborhood. No matter what the living situation the intention here is to build a community that would provide some level of safety and privacy for those who opt out of the mainstream technocratic world. I want to stress that this option is not necessarily about bailing on your home. As I will outline in the chapter on the Counter-Economic Underground Railroad, choosing to exit and build before the shit hits the fan might help your close friends and family down the line when it really matters. More on that later.

3. Apathy is Death - Of course, you are always free to do nothing. Perhaps you see what's on the horizon and decide that A) it's too late to stop the Technocracy, B) it's too much work to make an effort, or C) you are just trying to take care of your own family and live a peaceful life. I could go on, but you likely get the point. It's your life and you are not obligated to take any action upon learning of the Technocracy and the digital dystopia being built. However, I would warn that apathy today will only make life more difficult for the generations of the future. If we want to preserve and expand liberty and privacy for all people we are going to have to take action in realistic and tangible ways.

Of course we could brainstorm a dozen more options, but generally I believe all plans can be sorted into one of these three categories. For those choosing Option 1 it is important to understand that deciding to stay put while attempting to opt-out of the Technocracy will involve breaking the law at some point. As the State continues the push for mandatory biometrics (retina, fingerprint, and face scanning) and social credit systems are adopted widely, it will become increasingly difficult to operate your life without directly violating the

Technocratic State's orders. The trick is to determine the potential risk vs the potential benefit.

As Konkin once wrote, *"trade risk for profit."* With the understanding that every decision we make is economic (whether it relates to money or not), Konkin recognized that choosing to violate the commands of the State was a risk that could result in a profit in the form of an increase in liberty in one form or another. So when you choose not to report all of your income on your taxes in order to save money for your family you are trading a risk for a benefit. In a similar way if or when the State issues mandatory vaccination orders, mandatory retina scanning, mandatory micro chipping, or any other mandatory program you will have a choice. You can submit to these programs out of fear of punishment or damage to reputation, or you can consciously choose to opt-out of these systems. There will be risks and there will be benefits. It is up to you to decide what is best for you and your family.

In his unfinished book *Counter-Economics* Samuel Konkin described what he calls Low-Profile and High-Profile Counter-Economics, two different tactics available to those who seek to opt-out of invasive systems. While Low-Profile Counter-Economics involves discreetly opting-out of the Technocracy, High-Profile is more in your face.

"High-Profile Counter-Economics deals with a particular area of State coercion by calling attention to his or her victimization. The more noise, the better. The famed Chicago 8 used publicity to keep themselves out of prison for years—even after their convictions.

Civil disobedients trust public pressure to keep them out of jail or to minimize their penalties. Indeed, the State's enforcers are wary of creating martyrs. The very concept of martyr exhibits the power of Information; what is a martyr but a corpse with a good story?

High-Profile Counter-Economists have higher risks because they are so easy to detect. They gain the advantage of additional information flow—from themselves to the rest of the market. To the extent they succeed, they become inspirational."

Konkin said those who pursued both Low- and High-Profile simultaneously could do so through a third category: The Counter-Economic Community. Konkin notes the benefits of having allies who are also participating in the counter-economy and opting-out of the Technocracy. This is why it is going to be important to form some level of a community as a mutual support network that allows for a life "off the grid." Konkin wrote:

"One may pursue any degree of notoriety (or, to put it another way, freely advertise one's services) within the community of fellow counter-economists while not informing the State, its agents, and, of course, its informers. To do that, one needs to control the flow of information about oneself."

One of the great insights outlined by Konkin in *Counter-Economics* is the importance of controlling the flow of information about yourself, *"in particular, the information flow from you to the State."* Konkin says the two obvious ways to escape the State's notice is to not exist and *"if you do exist, don't tell anyone about it."* The goal then is to reduce interaction with the State and/or private companies who want to scan your face, record your life, and force you to submit.

There are many ways to approach this goal. For example, Konkin noted that some aspiring counter-economists have chosen to *"cut themselves off from contact with anyone who might get to know them, get and stay off all mailing lists, operate through cash and never use banks, and even avoid legal residences, living in trailers as nomads or on neglected land in caves or makeshift structures."* While this may sound extreme to some, for a brief period in the 1960s these individuals promoted the philosophy of Vonu, or invulnerability toward coercion, and attempted to avoid all contact with the State. Tom Marshall, aka Ryo, was the main proponent of Vonu and often wrote about finding his version of freedom by completely opting out of society and living solitary in the wilderness or in his RV. Some of those who choose Option 2 may be interested in Vonu, but in my experience most people seem interested in living with their family or in a community of like-minded people who do not want to submit to the digital prison rather than alone. If any lesson is learned from the proponents of Vonu it is that opting-out is absolutely possible whether in a high-profile counter-economic manner or an extreme low-profile Vonu lifestyle. (For those interested in a deeper look at Vonu I recommend checking out *Vonu: A Strategy for Self-Liberation* by Shane Radliff)

Both Konkin and Ryo warned of the difficulties facing those seeking liberation and privacy within the city. However, in the increasingly interconnected digital world in which we live privacy can be difficult even in rural areas. Whether you choose to Hold Down The Fort and build community in the city or town you live or Exit and Build your community in a new location, the goal is to limit interaction with the Technocratic State. This is where we can learn from the Vonu enthusiasts who talked about "interfacing" with the rest of society on a selective basis.

Konkin says one way to interface with the "overground or establishment economy" (or mainstream world in general) is to create a fictitious identity who takes the risks. In this case you can drop this identity at a moment's notice if necessary. In the digital world it is easy to create an alternative persona online, but it is more difficult to be truly disconnected from your online identity. In my journalism career I have seen governments track people with phones, cameras, computers and GPS and even crack encryption. As Konkin notes, *"if the State's agents are closing in on this alter-ego, as long as you wear the guise they are closing in on you."* Additionally, anything you gained while using the false identity—accounts, contacts, and property—would be lost.

Konkin viewed false personalities as valuable, but ultimately he believed it was necessary to categorize your information flow into a system of layers. For example, at one layer you must reveal some information in order to interact with the rest of the world. This information can include *"that you have a product or service, how much it will cost, what you will accept in payment, how you can be contacted, and when are you or it available. If there are multiple payments, credit arrangements, repeat business, and post-sale follow-up involved, still more information must flow from you."*

When purchasing or selling a product, working for an employer, or traveling you will leave a digital paper trail and also are more likely to face the biometric tools of the Technocracy. Again, if you live in a major city (or even a small city) and choose Option 1 these are challenges you will have to face. In the U.S., China, UK, France, Australia, India, etc., CCTV cameras connected to 24-hour "Real Time Crime Centers" and "Fusion Centers" keep civilians in most major cities under heavy surveillance. Increasingly these cameras are being outfitted with facial recognition software. To combat this threat there are two main strategies that I call "Be Invisible" and "Seek & Destroy."

Be Invisible

If your goal is to remain low-profile and Be Invisible there are few actions you can take immediately:

- Stop carrying cell phones everywhere you go
- Stop using GPS
- Delete social media accounts and apps that track you
- Stop using credit and debit cards
- Cancel your bank account (use a credit union if you need to store your funds)
- Stop working jobs in the mainstream economy
- Stop paying taxes

Now, obviously some of these options are going to be extreme for some people. It's all about the level of information flow you are willing to accept. Some people can't quit their day jobs or cancel their bank accounts or delete their social media accounts. I get it. This means there will be some level of information about you available to those with the money and the desire to buy it. There's nothing inherently wrong with this. Perhaps your major concern is simply making sure the cell phones and home assistants are not listening to you all the time. So you choose not to buy an Alexa, Echo, etc. and you choose to only turn your cell phone on when you need it. These are personal choices and they will differ with every individual. The point is that you are in control of the data flowing out from you.

When it comes to the digital world there is still an incredible value to understanding how to use encryption. The number of digital devices you use directly correlates with your level of privacy and liberty. If your wifi, phone, laptop, tablet, etc. are all operating without any type of encryption you are at the mercy of all manner of bad actors. There is also the matter of off the shelf computers being built with backdoors which allow government and private companies to access your data without a problem. Of course, using VPN's (Virtual Private Networks) is valuable but documents leaked by Edward Snowden proved that the U.S. NSA can crack these as well. One tool discussed by Konkin that is still valuable is public-key cryptography. We don't have the space here to elaborate further, but I recommend learning more about cryptographic privacy and Pretty Good Privacy (PGP) encryption.

I will add one final caveat about digital communication: assume someone can see it. Even if you are using encrypted messenger apps that promise to destroy your messages instantly it is a safe assumption that the American and Chinese governments can access it if they so choose. All digital communications can be collected, stored, and analyzed if someone wants it done. Always operate as if someone else can see what you are sending. If something sensitive needs to be communicated then say it in person in a room without computers, phones, smart devices, or digital home assistants.

There are also some practical ways to fight back. In 2019 there were several stories reporting that activists had found ways to fight back against the surveillance grid. In Chile, activists pointed lasers at drones observing their behavior from the skies during massive anti-government protests. Hundreds of lasers pointing directly at the drone caused it to malfunction and fall to the floor with a thunderous applause and cheers from the people. In Hong Kong, protesters also used lasers to fight against surveillance. To fight against facial recognition cameras the activists began using high-powered lasers aimed at cameras and police. As the corporate-state advances it is likely they will discover how to avoid falling prey to simple lasers, so it is important that the people are always looking for (or creating) advances in technology that can counter the State.

Some companies and designers have recently begun advertising clothing, face paint, glasses, and even certain hair styles that might be able to bypass facial recognition. Berlin-based artists Adam Harvey has launched two different projects seeking to overwhelm and confuse facial recognition systems. His Hyperface project involves printing clothing with eyes, mouths, and other facial features in an attempt to deceive the software. Harvey also worked on the CV Dazzle project which sought to use makeup and hairstyle to interfere with the machines. Other artists have suggested that clothing that is shiny, reflective, and can bounce light as well as military style camo could disrupt the facial recognition nightmare and render you invisible.

Of course the most practical way to protect your face is to cover it. There are several options available for those interested including paper masks, the infamous Guy Fawkes ("Anonymous") mask, and 3D printed faces designed to give you another identity altogether. However, in China the State has made masks illegal and seeks to punish anyone who would obscure their identity. This has not stopped intrepid activists from continuing to use facial covers, but again the point is that if you want to protect your privacy it will likely involve breaking the law. If a law violates our right to liberty or privacy, then it is the law itself which is unjust and it should be ignored. However, it should be noted that in a world full of facial recognition cameras someone with a mask will surely stand out and be detected within moments. The less attention you bring to yourself the better.

Seek & Destroy

Before we go any further please note that this information is for educational and research purposes. You are fully responsible for your actions. Now for those who are dissatisfied with simply avoiding the invasive technology and playing a digital game of cat and mouse the Seek & Destroy option might better suit your needs.

We can look to Hong Kong again for another example. In August 2019, activists targeted "smart lamps" that the local government says are used to collect data on traffic, weather, and air quality. Activists feared the smart street lights had been equipped with facial recognition software so they tied ropes around the poles and pulled them down to the ground. There are about 50 smart lampposts installed around Hong Kong, all of which have cameras and sensors. These are the same kind of smart lamps being installed in "Smart Cities" around the world.

Again, I recognize this might sound extreme to some, but I have met a diverse crowd of people who have expressed that if the technology comes to their neighborhoods they *will* tear it down. This brings us to the topic of monkeywrenching, a form of direct action originally popularized by elements of the radical environmental movement, specifically Earth First! and the Earth Liberation Front (ELF). Dave Foreman co-founder of Earth First! outlined the tactics of monkeywrenching in his book *Ecodefense: A Field Guide to Monkeywrenching*. Foreman's book itself was inspired by Edward Abey's book *The Monkey Wrench Gang* which tells the story of four individuals who used sabotage to protest environmental damage in the Southwestern United States. Between 1992 and 2007, the Earth Liberation Front began sabotaging construction projects that threatened wild lands and forests. Their tactics included tree sitting, non-violent blockades, civil disobedience, and disrupting machinery.

One need not agree with the philosophy or even the cause of the ELF and Earth First! to recognize that monkeywrenching can be applied to a number of different causes. I would say what the Hong Kong protesters did to the smart lamps was monekywrenching in defense of privacy and liberty. As always, you decide the risks vs the potential benefits. To those who are uncomfortable with the idea of destruction, **remember that every ending breathes a new beginning**. We can build a world that respects privacy and individual liberty on top of the ashes of the Technocratic State's facial recognition cameras.

These are just a handful of suggestions on strategy and tactics for maintaining some level of privacy and liberty. As Konkin correctly noted the fight for privacy is a *"dynamic, evolving system. It is a non-violent form of an arms race where one side cracks the code and the other develops a new system to top the old one."*

Digital technology is a tool and like every tool it can be used for good or for harm. In the hands of the technocrats digital tech is used for control, spying, social engineering, manipulation, censorship, and propaganda. In the hands of free people technology can be used to heal, empower, educate, and build a better

45

world. However, this better world will not happen without a conscious effort to build it. We also need a healthy skepticism towards emerging technologies which are sold as the panacea to humanity's turmoil. Whether you choose to stay put and build in your town or vacate the State and build elsewhere, it will be necessary to participate in some level of community if only for survival. Our best chance for survival is to band together with others who choose to opt out of the digital future and form new communities which respect privacy and liberty.

6. The Counter-Economic Community: Freedom Cells

Throughout his writing Samuel Konkin refers to the benefits of existing with an agorist, or counter-economic community. Although Konkin never completed a detailed outline of how this community might operate he does make a few helpful references. In the outline to *Counter-Economics*, under the heading "Chapter Fifteen: Psychology Counter-Economics," Konkin wrote:

"Mutual Reinforcement—Going beyond individual self-reliance and self-acceptance, the concept of individuals working together counter-economically, developing trust and honest interdependence, will finally be developed (after popping up briefly all over the book). Beyond relationships and affinity groups, we come logically to the idea of an active sub-society and/or Movement of Counter-Economists—and that brings us to Part II."

Unfortunately, Konkin never wrote Part 2 or elaborated on the community angle. The reality is that whether you choose to Hold Down the Fort or Exit and Build community is going to be necessary to survive the Technocracy. I have spent the last few years developing the concept of Freedom Cells, which I believe lines up perfectly with the counter-economic vision. Freedom Cells are peer-to-peer groups made up of seven to nine people (with eight being ideal) organizing themselves in a decentralized manner with the collective goal of asserting the sovereignty of group members through peaceful resistance and the creation of alternative institutions. Freedom Cells (FCs) can be seen as a very specific type of mutual aid group where Agorism and Counter-Economics play a key role. The name comes as a response to State propaganda around "Terror Cells." I am consciously choosing to reclaim the language and build cells that spread freedom. Also, FCs act like cells in a body that are performing important tasks individually while also serving the goals of the larger organism. From this view, every FC is playing a vital role in spreading counter-economic activity while also forming a part of the larger network that will foster exchange of ideas and products between different cells.

The number of eight participants is drawn from the research of Bob Podolsky and his book *Flourish!: An Alternative to Government and Other Hierarchies.* Podolsky is the protege of researcher John David Garcia who spent twenty years researching how to maximize the creativity of a group of people working together on a joint project. After performing hundreds of experiments, he came up with an optimized model based on groups of eight, which he called an octet or octologue. The idea is that a shortage of individuals would leave the group limited in capability, but with too many people the group is bogged down with disorganization and a lack of focus. Podolsky recommends forming octologues made up of four men and four women guided by specific ethical tenets. Although Freedom Cells are also promoted as groups of eight individuals collaborating together, they differ from octologues in that they are heavily focused on decentralization. While Bob Podolsky has outlined a detailed vision of how an octologue should operate, I hope to provide examples of applications for FCs without telling other FCs how to operate. The needs of each community will naturally differ. Beyond a general agreement to respect each other's right to be free of coercion I believe FCs should not be monopolized by the vision of a single cell. I caution the reader to remember that these ideas are a guide and not the final word on the literally limitless possibilities.

In the beginning, individuals can work together to accomplish goals such as every group member having three months' worth of storable food, encrypted communication, a bug out (or Exit and Build) plan, and ensuring participants have access to firearms (or some form of self-defense) and know how to use them safely and proficiently. All the while cell members make themselves readily available to render mutual aid to their cell in whatever form that may be necessary. After you have established seven - nine people within a FC each individual should be encouraged to then go on their own and start another FC, especially if the original members are not living in close proximity to one another. Living reasonably close to each other will allow for a quick response time in emergency situations. Once again, every member of the FCs should be encouraged to start additional cells.

Eventually the original cell would be connected to seven or nine additional cells through individual members for a total of 70-90 people. Imagine the strength and influence these cells could exert once connected in the digital world via

FreedomCells.org and in the physical world where possible. The creation of the Freedom Cell Network also serves as a social network for travelers looking to do business in the counter-economy with other like-minded people. Through building and supporting alternatives such as local food networks, health services, mutual defense groups, and peer-to-peer economies and communication networks, FCs will be better able to disconnect and decouple themselves from the Technocratic State. Once groups become large enough in numbers it becomes quite possible for participants to opt-out en masse and to secure their liberty.

This is the model we followed within The Houston Free Thinkers activist community and The Free Thinker House community space. We began by building gardens and selling the crops via the Nextdoor community. We also sold juice and kombucha tea made using fruits harvested from trees of neighbors who understood our goals. We started with a small group of about three to four people meeting and discussing the goals and themes of our cell. The goal is to have skills and knowledge diffused throughout the group. This way if one person leaves the group the knowledge is not taken from the cell. For example, knowing that every cell member can perform CPR, use encrypted communications, shoot a gun, or communicate the counter-economic message may be important for your cell. Obviously, certain individuals will be more skilled or knowledgeable in some areas, but there are foundational skills and information that should be common among all cell members.

Our group also used the structure to educate each other on specific topics of interest. Perhaps your FC meets and agrees to learn everything available on permaculture or a particular philosophical concept. You can then choose to divide the topic up among your cell and return two weeks later to educate each other. Perhaps your cell joins the Cell411 app and responds to emergency alerts in your community. Several cells could join together to cop watch or actively resist and disarm violent police or other agents of the State. A Freedom Cell could connect with other cells for a covertly organized guerrilla gardening action. With the constant barrage of fake news coming from the establishment media a FC could quickly research and debunk incoming propaganda. FCs can organize alternative exchange networks that encourage local artisans and entrepreneurs to sell their unregulated crafts and accept alternative currencies. In a "Shit Hits the Fan" scenario, FCs could have prearranged bug out locations stocked with supplies. If several FCs were equally prepared, you now find yourself with a small community of empowered individuals as opposed to being forced to defend yourself alone.

When it comes to dealing with the Technocracy, FC members can make commitments to limit the amount of information which is communicated via digital technology, saving important conversations for face-to-face. Additionally, members can share tips for evading the watchful eyes of the State. However, the real value of using Freedom Cells to build the counter-economic community is strength in numbers. If your decision not to adopt the mandatory biometrics or social credit goes from frowned upon to illegal you will face punishment for choosing not to participate. As we noted earlier, the goal of social credit schemes is to socially engineer society to be blind, dumb, and obedient followers of the Technocracy. The State is going to use the Technocracy to promote the idea that anyone who chooses to opt-out is the problem. Even the most strident individualist will find it hard to survive "off the grid" once the Technocracy is complete. Of course, the social credit score will also discourage friends and family from associating with those who have been blacklisted.

The solution is to collaborate with other individuals and families who choose not to submit. The reasons for opting out will vary from person to person—some may opt-out to avoid mandatory vaccinations, others to practice their religious beliefs in peace, while still others will exit to protect the privacy of their future progeny. Frankly, if the choice is mandatory obedience to the Smart Grid or a life "outside" of mainstream society, it will take a coordinated effort by many determined individuals to create a world of networked communities where individuals can thrive, raise their families, conduct business, and trade while still living free. I believe the concept of FCs can help those of us who will do anything to be free from the web of the Technocracy.

In conclusion, I offer these "12 Tips For Building Freedom Cells" as a starting point for launching your group. Please adapt these to the specific needs of your community:

1. Understand Your Motivation - I find it valuable for every person considering starting a cell/circle/hub to know why they are pursuing such a goal. What are your motivations and interests? Knowing this before you start a group will save you time. Finding ways to opt-out of the Technocracy is an obvious goal, but what else drives you?

2. Identify Potential Candidates - Are they mentally, physically, spiritually sound for your goals?

3. Discuss Common Themes - What are the driving forces bringing the group together?

4. Identify Strengths and Weaknesses - Take an honest look at the strengths and weaknesses of each individual as well as the group as a whole.

5. Evaluate Desired Level of Freedom vs Security - Every individual may have a different desired level of freedom and as such will have different aims and acceptability of risks. When it comes to the Technocracy this is especially important to remember. How free do you really want to be? How much privacy do you want to keep? What will you do to attain such a goal?

6. Set Short Term and Long Term Goals - What can your cell accomplish in three months? Six months? A year? Set goals as a group and hold each other accountable.

7. Mindfulness Training - Incorporate practices like Nonviolent Communication Training and group meditation into your cell.

8. Accomplish Goals - Document each goal successfully met by the cell or individual members.

9. Ongoing Group Education, Communication - Continuously expand your cell's knowledge, skills, and supplies.

10. Promote/Market Goals and Accomplishments - Use the power of social media (when safe) and marketing to let the world know how much more prosperous you are in the counter-economy.

11. Identify Strategies For Creating Income/Independence - Leverage the power and number of your cell to create counter-economic income that cannot be taxed by the State.

12. Network with Other Cells - The key to opting-out of the Technocratic State is building the counter-economic community. This means not only your immediate community of allies but the larger network of cells in your city, state/province, nation, and the global community. It is up to you to make an effort to network with other activists and free thinkers.

7. The Counter-Economic Underground Railroad

For the last two years, I have focused on developing potential solutions for liberating hearts and minds from the grip of the Technocracy. I have come to the conclusion that whichever path you choose to take proper precautions and emergency plans are necessary. The cliche *hope for the best, prepare for the worst* applies here. While I have offered suggestions to those who choose to Hold Down the Fort, it is imperative that some individuals choose to Exit and Build in the event that the "fort" collapses. These forward thinking individuals may choose to move out of major cities to rural areas with less invasive practices or move to a nearby region with relatively more liberty and privacy. The goal is to establish a network of free communities that could serve as safe havens for refugees of the Technocratic State. This is what I call the "Counter-Economic Underground Railroad," or simply the Underground Railroad.

This Counter-Economic Underground Railroad is modeled after the original "Underground Railroad" of the American colonial era. In the late 1700s, former slaves, abolitionists, and sympathetic civilians formed a decentralized network of safe houses that allowed slaves to escape from bondage. Most of the freed slaves made their way north to Canada but there were also safe houses helping people escape south to Mexico. It has been estimated that as many as 1,000 slaves escaped per year between 1850 and 1860. The Underground Railroad was inherently counter-economic because under the Fugitive Slave Act of 1793 law enforcement in free states were required to help slaveholders recapture runaway slaves. Fortunately, many officials had the good sense to ignore the unjust law and help former slaves make their way to freedom. This was a conscious decision to violate the State's demands and trade risk for a perceived benefit.

In the notes to his unfinished chapters "Smuggling Counter-Economics" and "Human Counter-Economics," SEK3 mentions the Underground Railroad as an example of people smuggling. In "Smuggling Counter-Economics" he writes, *"Smuggling 'people' is introduced, to be used in the 'Human Counter-Economics' Chapter,* **with underground railway of the Civil War period."**

It is important to note there is a difference between smuggling a person voluntarily and involuntary human trafficking done under the threat of violence.

Smuggling typically involves choosing to transport goods which the State has deemed illegal or avoiding taxes on the transportation of said goods. People or human smuggling involves one individual paying another to be smuggled across international borders. While smuggling typically involves some form of contractual agreement that ends upon arrival to the destination, human trafficking involves the use of force, abduction, fraud, or coercion. This is often used to induce forced labor or sexual exploitation. Simply put, smuggling becomes trafficking when the element of force or coercion is introduced. Under Konkin's counter-economic theory, human smuggling is legitimate because it does not involve the initiation of violence or coercion. In "Human Counter-Economics" SEK3 provides a little more detail of his vision:

*"Underground Railway slaves moved counter-economically, variants of it still in use; Refugees covers Counter-Economics of freeing people from greater tyranny, **Minority groups are covered here first, how they survive in hostile societies, and the sub- societies they form, usually overwhelmingly counter-economic..."***

Although we don't have the finished work, it is interesting that Konkin mentions minority groups and *"how they survive in hostile societies, and the sub-societies they form."* In the age of the Technocratic State those choosing to opt-out will be the minority groups surviving in hostile societies. The sub-societies we form could be the free communities which keep the flame of liberty burning into the future. Imagine the Freedom Cell Network expanding to both urban and rural environments around the world. Those who stay in the cities do what they can to combat the Technocracy and educate others of the dangers. Those who exit build communities which opt-out of various levels of invasive technology (based on their preferences) and also educate others about the benefits of unplugging. The two strategies work together to pull as many minds out of the technocratic matrix as possible.

Regardless of whether you see value to counter-economic theory there are practical lessons to be learned from the Underground Railroad. The individuals who chose to open their homes to runaway slaves made a conscious decision to risk arrest and imprisonment so they could help a fellow human being. The police and government officials who disobeyed the State joined the counter-economy when they realized that doing what was right was more important than doing what was legal. The allies who smuggled former slaves across international borders also risked their freedom for a just cause. These are the same decisions I believe many of us will face in the coming years as the Technocratic State continues to grow.

The individuals who choose to Exit and Build now can purchase land, build housing, and lay the foundation of a more free society. While this will initially serve to provide for their own families, if the shit hits the fan the Underground Railroad will help slaves of the Technocracy escape to these communities. This is the role I am choosing to take. I do not believe my place of birth (the United States) is salvageable. I do not see this as abandoning ship or giving up hope but rather I am consciously choosing to build the future I desire with the understanding that others may need help in the near future. I believe by exiting the city, moving to a less invasive region of the world, and building on land I will find my inner peace and have an opportunity to help others. This might not be the particular role you choose, but there are other ways we can each be of service.

As in the original Underground Railroad we will need sympathetic individuals within the hostile society who are willing to house and transport those seeking safety. We will need low-level employees of the State willing to take a bribe or simply turn a blind eye to the Counter-Economic Underground Railroad. We will need "white hat" hackers willing to create technological tools tocombat the omnipresent eyes and ears of the smart grid. We will need individuals who leave behind comfort to develop the network of free communities that might soon house refugees of the Technocracy. Finally, we will need organizers who can help connect each of these individuals in as decentralized a manner as possible.

I do not claim to know exactly how this Counter-Economic Underground Railroad will develop. The only thing I know is that it must develop as soon as possible. If we choose to sit by idly while the Technocratic State comes into view we are abandoning future generations of our human family. If you are reading these words you have the opportunity to be a part of the solution. **The only way we will make it through the digital dystopia is to put aside minor differences and build the world we know is possible.**

8. Final Thoughts on Surviving the Digital Dystopia

In late 2009 I began questioning the world around me and wondering who was running the show. I consumed as much material as I could find on the history of government, banks, the ruling class, and power. For a moment I was convinced that the end of the world, a government collapse, a police state, or something of that sort was coming. Over time my fears receded as I took a more reasoned look at the world around me and also took note of the many positive advances unfolding in that world. Unfortunately, as I write these words my fears of an impending doom have returned. Only now I see the impending threat coming from what I am calling the Technocratic State.

This State is unlike any other previously seen in humanity's history. There is an elitist, totalitarian ruling class made up of the technocrats and mad scientists combined with digital technology not available to past totalitarian regimes. This does not bode well for the future of liberty for all people. The modern conception of liberty is barely 300 years old itself and it appears as if humanity may have trouble maintaining and expanding such a necessary principle. Apparently humanity is still deciding whether concepts like privacy and liberty will continue to thrive.

Will liberty expand to all lands of the Earth or will the tyrants continue to reign? I don't pretend to know exactly how the future is going to turn out, but I do know the outcome will be determined by those who choose to step up and take action. The direction will depend on the values and the principles of those who get engaged and seek solutions. Those who sit on the sidelines will merely be cogs in someone else's machine. The time for passivity has come to an end. **If you do not want to lose privacy and eventually all liberty you must act to protect yourself and your loved ones.**

The Technocracy is coming into full view and everyday it becomes more clear that the masses will swallow the poison without hesitation. Opting-out of the conveniences and pleasures of the smart grid will not be a popular choice. Saying no to mandatory biometric systems will involve some level of risk. However, it may soon be necessary to make these decisions to preserve your privacy and liberty. I have attempted to outline why I believe Samuel E. Konkin's theory of

Counter-Economics can be applied to the battle against the totalitarian surveillance state. Counter-Economics provides a philosophical foundation to the simple act of saying "no" to immoral or unjust state rules and doing what you must to thrive.

The facts are all there: when the State moves to prohibit an activity or a substance they create a counter-economy of people who will voluntarily choose to violate the State's demands and do what they feel is necessary to survive and thrive. This counter-economy is one of the largest economies in the world and none of it is controlled by a centralized authority. The power of Counter-Economics lies in recognizing the potential of a mass opting-out of systems that do not align with our values and are inherently immoral. Just as in the original Underground Railroad I am calling for the creation of safe houses, the transporting of refugees, and the conscious objection to laws which try to criminalize those who help runaways. The "conductors" of the original Underground Railroad did what they knew was right because it mattered more than blindly following words on pieces of paper.

We should take inspiration from this example of counter-economic activity and consciously opt-out of the technocratic control grid. If we form Freedom Cells which promote counter-economic activity and encourage skepticism towards the Technocracy we may have a chance to form a competing society of free communities that choose to reject various levels of invasive digital technology. **We cannot face this monumental task alone. It is of extreme importance that we find a way to form alliances and coalitions in the interest of saving our collective liberty.**

I believe opting-out of the Technocratic State should go hand in hand with opting-out of the military-industrial complex (MIC), the central banking system, the school system, the corporate-media complex, and the pharmaceutical complex. This will not be easy or even possible for all people in all situations. **Do what you can, where you can.** Refer back to Vertical and Horizontal Agorism when you need ideas for opting-out of a wide range of institutions and organizations that do not represent your interests. I also recommend spending time going over my explanations of the Hold Down the Fort and Exit and Build strategies to see where you think your path may lead you.

It is ultimately up to each individual to decide their future and the totality of each of our choices will set the path for all of humanity. I have attempted to understand how to motivate others to take action and I have found that leading by example is the best way to inspire others. We need not all take the exact same route to achieve success. In fact, the more diverse the field of individuals employing the counter-economic ethic the better off we will be. Each of us will be inspired and motivated by different stimuli, and we will each reach and inspire different people.

Not only are we all motivated differently but our habits and lifestyles will also shape our ability to be free from the Technocratic State. The level of privacy and liberty you maintain in the coming years will be decided by your willingness to change, adapt, and abandon habits which weaken your ability to be free of systems of oppression. This struggle between what you want (liberty) and your actions (a variable dependent on you) decides whether your desires become reality or remain a fantasy.

Level of Freedom Desired + Willingness to Change = Your Actual Experience of Freedom

I call this the Freedom Formula—a simple equation in which your level of freedom desired plus your willingness to change and adapt equals your experience of liberty and privacy. To determine the best path for yourself it is important to understand what your goals are and what your ideal vision of liberty and privacy looks like. This is part one of the formula. Only after you clearly identify what you want and what you do not want can you begin to ask what you are willing to do to achieve this goal. While some might call this a sacrifice, the reality is we have long been trading our invaluable privacy and liberty for convenience and pleasure. Do you value the convenience of skipping the line at the airport in exchange for your faceprint more than you value privacy? Is it worth losing privacy just so you can download the latest apps and trends?

As you imagine the answers to these questions I humbly request that you take a moment to consider the consequences of apathy and complacency. Future generations have never been more dependent on those living today to correct the course of humanity. We have reached the point where children are growing up without any sense of a world without the Internet, without smart phones, and without a smart grid. These generations will likely lack a true understanding of the value and importance of privacy because they are being raised in a culture and time where privacy is hardly a concern. As Artifical Intelligence improves, the 5G Smart Grid goes live, and the Internet of Things springs into existence we are going to face difficult decisions regarding privacy. If we choose to be the ones who planned ahead, opted out, and formed free communities we can leave future generations a world that respects the principles of liberty and privacy. While my optimism is lacking as of late, I do believe there is still time to lay the foundation for the Counter-Economic Underground Railroad and build the better world we know is possible.

Part 3:
Counter-Economics:
From the Back Alleys to the Stars
by Samuel E. Konkin III

Originally Published as Digital Edition: November, 2018.
Published by KoPubCo at Smashwords
KoPubCo is the publishing division of The Triplanetary Corporation
5904-A Warner Ave., Ste. 164 Huntington Beach, California 92649-4689
Website: kopubco.com | email: info@kopubco.com

Samuel E. Konkin III began developing his philosophy of Agorism and the strategy of counter-economics in the early 1970s before writing the seminal *New Libertarian Manifesto*. The book laid out the black market-anarchist platform in all its glorious detail. Konkin's second book, *An Agorist Primer*, was released after his death in 2004. The work further illuminated the path to what Konkin called *New Libertarianism* or *Agorism*. Before his death Konkin was intending to release another book known as *Counter-Economics.* Konkin envisioned the book as an academic tome that would rival Marx's *Communist Manifesto*.

Unfortunately, the book was never completed and Konkin's vision for the release was not realized. Thanks to Konkin,s friend Victor Koman, what survives of the book has now been released to the public in digital format. After hearing that Konkin had an unfinished and previously unseen book that was to be released, I decided I would "finish" the work as a sort of *thank you* to the original agorist for his effort to demonstrate the effectiveness of the economy that exists outside the tyrannical grasp of The State. Upon reading the completed six chapters and the outline to the entire book I became overjoyed at the possibility of bringing the book to life.

However, the book you hold in your hands is not the same vision Konkin outlined. I do not know if I am capable of creating a book that would satisfy Konkin's ambitious plan. Rather than attempting to recreate *Counter-Economics* as Konkin described, I decided to take Konkin's final work and update it to make it relevant to the 21st century and beyond. I believe Konkin's essays and my additions are key information for any individual or community interested in participating in counter-economic activity as a way to create more freedom in their lives. I give all credit to Samuel E. Konkin for laying down the foundation on which myself and many other counter-economists build.

I have included Konkin's original introduction and finished chapters as well as his personal notes for unwritten chapters. The following chapters make up six of the ten SEK3 wrote before he died. The other four have not been located as of January 2020. I present them to you as they were written by Konkin and edited by Victor Koman. Taken together these chapters illustrate a wealth of evidence for Konkin's theories regarding the power of the counter-economy. Upon reading this evidence the reader should ask the next obvious question—*what do we do about it?*

Konkin argued that all that was necessary was to raise the consciousness of the average person to recognize the opportunities that wait in the untaxed, unregulated counter-economy. If a mass of principled, consistent individuals resisted the extortion of the State and moved their energy into the counter-economy the State would become impotent. From the 1980s until his death in 2004 Konkin recognized some of the earliest evidence of the success of the counter-economy. As we head into the 2020s the evidence is even greater than Konkin might have imagined. Yet once again we are confronted with the question—*what do we do about it?*

Do we take the evidence before us and use it to inform our actions as any reasonable person might? Or do we ignore the obvious solution in favor of continuing to play the political divide and conquer game? The choice is yours, my friends.

- Derrick Broze

Background

(The following note was written by award-winning author Victor Koman, PhD. It was originally published as the afterword to the ePub Edition of *Counter-Economics: From Back Alleys to the Stars,* the inspiration for *How to Opt-Out of the Technocratic State)*

The author of Counter-Economics, Samuel Edward Konkin III, died February 23, 2004 at the age of 56. He left his original manuscript with me in the hopes that a three-time Prometheus Award recipient and publisher (KoPubCo Books) would shepherd the book to publication, much as I had with Konkin's New Libertarian Manifesto (KoPubCo, 1983 & 2006) and the posthumously published introductory book An Agorist Primer (KoPubCo, 2008). The latter manuscript only required a light amount of updating, which allowed it to be published fairly quickly (by libertarian standards) after his death.

Counter-Economics, on the other hand, proved to be a greater challenge. The manuscript, written around 1984-85, consisted only of the first six chapters out of twenty in his outline (although four more chapters are rumored to exist somewhere in digital form, but have yet to be found). Moreover, extensive quotes from contemporary news and magazine sources constituted a significant portion of the manuscript. Because these references are now dated — for example, the Soviet Union's underground economy provided him with voluminous illustrations of statist economics gone utterly awry and Venezuela, the current poster-child for socialism's horrors, had yet to begin its collapse — finishing the book would have required a thorough re-application of Counter-Economics to a world a third of a century removed from that of the original manuscript.

The world has changed significantly since 1985 (with the proviso plus c'est la même chose): the collapse of the Soviet Union, due in no small part to Counter-Economics; the rise of Islamic terrorism; the return to a war-based (or, at least, war-accommodating) establishment economy; the scattershot legalization (but not decriminalization) of marijuana; the privatization (however meager) of space travel; the explosion of both computer encryption power and hackers' ingenuity; the rise of digital currency à la Bitcoin; the ubiquity of surveillance systems; the abandonment of any vestige of mouthed support for Liberty by the elites of US political parties, corporate boards, and governments worldwide. All these events have only served to increase, not decrease, the size and scope of the Counter-Economy.

In re-reading the chapters for this edition, I found echoes of the past reverberating in the present — it turns out that even though the references are dated, the principals underpinning CounterEconomics are consistent and timely, and you will see how they apply to current events and how they can resolve today's controversies and guide tomorrow's choices in your own life and society at large.

Scanning the manuscript in was an immensely frustrating effort (in the mid-1990s, using OmniPage with a primitive scanner). Sam's aging IBM Executive proportional-space typewriter had a floating "t" key that caused an OCR spelling error in almost every word containing that letter, as well as a spacing error in nearly every word with an "o". I spent hours and hours (as I could manage) over the ensuing years correcting errors and making Sam's endnotes consistent with APA 6th Ed. standards.

Because the book proposal had already made the rounds to several publishers and been rejected, Sam never felt it worthwhile to put any more effort into a rewrite. When Sam gave me the manuscript (probably 1993 or so), he doubted its marketability almost a decade after its writing, but I told him I might be able to do something with it and he gave me his permission to do so.

I knew, however, that I would not be able to complete the book by my 1990s self without some academic underpinning. Over the ensuing 20 or so years, I completed four university degrees, from an Associate of Arts, through a BSIS and an MBA, to an IT PhD in Information Assurance and Security. I also published the aforementioned SEK3 books and republished a few of my own through KoPubCo. All that while working full time at my web-app development job, 1996–2014. Finally, I felt ready to complete Sam's magnum opus with the scholarship and ideological consistency it deserved.

However...

At the urging of fellow award-winning author J. Neil Schulman, I attempted to find some reference by Sam to the Counter-Economics manuscript in my e-mail logs for the 1990s. Searching a 32 Mb text file (saved back when a megabyte was a megabyte!), I found several. And in them, I discovered something I had forgotten over the decades. In one e-mail, dated 11/28/1999, Sam wrote:

Although my "unpublishable" book, Counter-Economics, was only half-written before I gave up trying to find a New York publisher back in the early 1980s (best reply was from one who said, "This is an example of the most immoral writing of the Libertarian Movement..." yeah!), I have around 10 chapters I could retype and put on the web.

In a post to the Left Libertarian List, dated 1/26/00, Sam wrote:

... I mentioned before ... that I had written ten chapters of a book called Counter-Economics back in the early 1980s; it was turned down by a dozen Establishment New York publishers, two citing the "extremist" ideas as the reason and the others less honest. Each chapter described a particular area of C-E with the effect building up chapter by chapter until the reader realizes that it covers all Human Action.

Victor Koman apparently scanned and OCRed the manuscript pages and at Christmas this year presented them to me as a present. If I keep getting encouragement ... I'll put them on line....

The upshot of this is that I had totally forgotten about this exchange with Sam. All these years, I'd been holding onto the ms. in the hope of completing it with a scholar's research and writing skills because I wanted to protect the work's integrity, only to (re)discover that Sam had been ready to release the manuscript as-is, 'way back in the previous millennium...

So here it is, The Incompleat Counter-Economics. I have no idea where the four Lost Chapters may be, but I will reissue the e-book with them if/when they become available. The only changes I made to the manuscript were the correction of a few typos, the rewording of an unclear sentence or two, and the aforementioned APA formatting of the chapter endnotes. Shortly after the publication of this e-book, KoPubCo will make available a free PDF of the actual manuscript pages, along with additional matter such as scans of the actual articles SEK3 referenced in this book. What you have in your hands right now, though, is the purest distillation of CounterEconomics and proto-Agorism, presented by the genius — Samuel Edward Konkin III — who went beyond Von Mises and beyond Rothbard to provide you with the knowledge, strategy, and tactics to free yourself, and society, too. —VK

Introduction: by Samuel Edward Konkin III

Are you reading a self-help book, a personal liberation manual, a financial advisory, an esoteric economics text, an anti-political platform, a muckraking history, a sensational exposé of underground life, or an anarchist cookbook? The answer is *all of the above.*

 That may sound confusing, but the main purpose of this writing is to extract unity from these topics usually unconnected in most minds today. I hope it will indeed amuse and excite the reader about another, accessible way of life, give new explanation to some of the vexing problems that beset our social life, and perhaps solve a few. Along the way, a few more burdens may be lifted off the back of many of the oppressed — especially those who have chosen to fight back. Above all, may some of you be moved to act — on your own behalf.

That is where it begins — with the self. If the individual has rights and chooses to exercise them in the teeth of organized, institutionalized opposition, Counter-Economics begins. One need not be an anarchist or even much of a libertarian to counter-economize — and most to date have not been. Yet if a socialist or fascist or even one devoid of ideology or thought learns and applies counter-economic acts, the purest libertarianism has been, to my mind, advanced.

To that end, I have deliberately left the philosophical implications of Counter-Economics to the end of the book. And to make sure you've found wading through the subject exciting enough to take a plunge into deeper theory, I've put the economics next to the end.

This is not meant to lure the resistant or to trap the unwary. This book is neither treatise nor manifesto; the author has those available elsewhere. *Counter-Economics* is meant to make Counter-Economics as accessible to as many as possible.

Up front, then, with the deep stuff in the back, here's what Counter-Economics is. Economics is the study and practice of human action involving voluntary exchange. Establishment "economics" is the presentation of explanations of human action in such a way as to benefit the establishment or ruling segment of society. The former is an attempt at science; the latter is conartistry. *Counter-Establishment Economics* is the study and practice of that part of human action committed in spite of the official legitimacy (government legislation) to the contrary.

As *counter-establishment culture* proved unwieldy in the 1960s and was shortened to *counterculture* — though not without subsequent misrepresentation of its aims — *counter-establishment economics* will be shortened to counter-economics. To avoid misrepresentation, what I refer to as Counter-Economics will be capitalized consistently and defined in this way:

Counter-Economics is the theory and practice of all human action neither accepted by the State nor involving any initiatory violence or threat of violence.

If this formulation appears a bit arcane, it is required explicitly to exclude murder and theft from Counter-Economics. Governments have a near-monopoly on murder (war) and theft (taxation and inflation) and we can leave the few freelance statists out to give us a sharp, clean distinction.

Given, then, the libertarian moral code of not harming your fellow-sentient, Counter-Economics is doing what you want, when you want, for your own good reasons. And, with that, we push the theory to the back and get ready to survey the field.

The focus of the book is to show the reader what Counter-Economics is. We'll look at it in every aspect of life in all parts of the globe and beyond. Black market; grey market; dissidence both foreign and domestic; tax resistance; economic feminism; underground schools and shopping centers; gold, silver, barter, and illegal aliens; creative computing and secure information systems; gun-running and Bible-smuggling; life extension and intelligence increase; self-fulfillment and psychiatric resistance; sensational exploits and cold, hard, historical revisionism; alteration of inner space and outer space — it's all here.

After seeing for yourself, and then understanding in full, if you wish to try it… you'll find that you already have! If you wish to expand your freedom, you'll undoubtedly find some new ideas. Most important to me, if you are already expanding your freedom and were concerned about its validity, you hopefully will see the picture in full and judge for yourself your rightness.

If any counter-economist changes her or his mind about giving up a life of free marketeering to return to the "straight," sick, statist society, this book will have half-fulfilled its purpose. And if others perceive her or him in a new, more sympathetic light, the other half is fulfilled.

And now on to real human action. — SEK3

1. Tax Counter-Economics

"A vast underground economy rivaling the entire output of Canada in size, involving as many as 20 million people and generating hundreds of billions of dollars in untaxed income, is thriving beneath America's economic mainstream.

"All told, more than half a trillion dollars a year — about one quarter of recorded output in the U.S. — is involved, according to some estimates. Even the most conservative judgments start at nearly 200 billion."

U.S. News & World Report Cover story, October 22, 1979

"There's something happening here. What it is ain't exactly clear…"

— Stephen Stills, "For What It's Worth" (recorded by Buffalo Springfield)

Something called the "Underground Economy" has been discovered by the large-circulation, "Establishment" media. The Los Angeles Times, for example, during the years that the author kept close watch, ran the following stories:

• July 17, 1979 — "100 Billion 'Underground Economy' Revealed" (Section IV, Pages 1 & 11).
"'Anybody who has looked at the subterranean economy will tell you it's very large,' Allen Voss of the General Accounting Office told the House Ways & Means oversight subcommittee.

"Officials describe the underground economy as consisting of persons who report less than they earn, including those who engage in bartering or work for cash only, and those who don't even bother to file a return."

• September 18, 1979 — "'Underground Economy' Comes Up for Air" (Part II, Page 5). Columnist Robert J. Samuelson complains, "Government agencies have a way of conferring respectability on ideas, and that's just what the Internal Revenue Service has done for the 'underground economy.' Until recently, this was just another random subject for newspaper and magazine stories. Now the IRS has delivered a heavy report estimating that perhaps one dollar in every ten

70

of income has gone underground, and is not reported for tax purposes. Suddenly we have a full-scale social problem."

• January 9, 1980 — "Money, a Question of Give and Take," subtitled "Tax Man Cheated Out of Billions" (Part IV, Page 5), leads off with "'I feel wonderful about not paying taxes,' says R. M. Jones. 'I don't like to support a paper-tiger government and I don't like taking care of people on welfare.'"

• April 2, 1980 — "Evasions of Billions of Dollars In Income Tax Feared," subtitled "U.S. Concerned Over Unreported Funds Flowing Into Overseas Bank Accounts" expands the concept internationally. "The abuse of so-called "offshore' accounts by wealthy Americans bent on tax evasion — as well as by narcotics traffickers, corporate bribe-payers, and others — has reached unprecedented proportions, according to many experts."

• April 7, 1980 — "On the Side of the Lawless," subtitled "Americans' Tolerance of Underground-Economy Tax Cheats Costs Them Billions," is an editorial attack by Times editorial writer Ernest Conine. Says he, "Most Americans are inclined to wink at such goings on. That isn't very smart, to say the least. The fellow who cheats on his income taxes, whether he's a carpet-layer or a multimillionaire businessman, is stealing from honest taxpayers just as surely as if he stuck a gun in their ribs."

• April 17, 1980 — "More and More Refusing to Pay Taxes," subtitled "Resisters and 'Patriots' Insist U.S. Has No Right to Levies" does not mention the "Underground Economy" anywhere (Part 1-C, Pages 7-8). Yet it begins, "A growing number of Americans are refusing to file income tax forms or to pay Uncle Sam another penny. Most of us spend several months a year working for the federal government, but the tax resisters have told the government, 'I quit.'" More on this anomaly later.

• April 18, 1980 — "Biggest Tax Swindle of Them All" headed a letter column in the Times responding to Conine. Six missives were printed, all critical of Conine's defense of taxation, though two supported taxation by offering an alternative, the Value-Added Tax or VAT. Two others contained this one-word sentence in riposte to Conine: "Nonsense!" Another said, "Conine's inept suggestion that we hire more auditors is asinine!"

• August 18, 1980 — "IRS Acts to Curb Rise in Tax Rebels," subtitled "Ranks Swell Despite Convictions," again does not mention any "Underground Economy." (Section l, Page 1)

• January 10, 1981 — "Churches May Be Auctioned Off," subtitled "15 Congregations Refusing to File State Tax Forms" expands the issue again from individuals and organized tax rebels to churches (Page 30, Part I). "At least 15 California fundamentalist churches involved in a growing revolt against filing tax forms are in danger of having their properties auctioned off by the State." Yet again, no "underground economy" is mentioned.

Nor is this confined to the L.A. Times or U.S. News. Jack Anderson's column of December 29, 1979, begins, "Honest American taxpayers are being ripped off by an ever-growing economic 'underground' of tax chiselers whose unpaid taxes must be made up by the law-abiding population. Estimates vary on the size of these tax guerrillas' annual depredations, but some experts believe that their illicit tax-free transactions make up as much as one-third of the total American economy. Perhaps the most alarming feature of this shadowy army of cheaters is that many of its recruits are not hardened underworld figures, but respected and seemingly respectable citizens."

Columnist Sylvia Porter, "Your Money's Worth," devoted three columns (November 10–12, 1980) to the "'Invisible' Underground Economy." She concludes apocalyptically, "Compliance must be the answer if we are to avoid the danger that our whole system will fall apart."

Perhaps her vision is not unwarranted. Zodiac News Service, August 1, 1980, sent out the following story:

(ZNS) The Internal Revenue Service recently decided to run a check on its own employees by auditing the personal income tax returns of 168 of its own auditors, who were selected at random.

72

The IRS reports that 110 of those audits are now complete, and that exactly half of the Service's own auditors made serious errors in their own personal returns.

Of the 55 inaccurate returns, 13 overpaid their taxes by an average of $129. The remaining 42, however, underpaid Uncle Sam by an average of $ 720. This $720 figure, incidentally, is more than double the public's average underpayment of around $340.

The IRS was going to expand its audit of its own auditors, but has since canceled that plan after the auditors labeled the scheme "outrageous," and "very, very unfair."

And the "threat" is not limited even yet. Thomas Brom, for Pacific News Service, November 28, 1980, in the article "America's Booming 'Outlaw' Economy — Jobs for Many, Protection For None," begins with this dire warning as an "Editor's Note": "The 'outlaw' or 'underground' economy, where cash pays the bill and the IRS is shunned, is growing by leaps and bounds, according to recent estimates. It has come to function as a kind of shadowy catch-all survival system and unofficial welfare program for the growing legions of unemployed. But while it offers survival for many, it provides little welfare and no worker protection, and it represents a serious threat to American unions, reports Thomas Brom, PNS economics editor."

Finally, nothing is a popular phenomenon if it's not reported in People magazine. So September 1979, page 30, a full-page photo of the General Accounting Office's Richard Fogel, captioned "If the government doesn't take action, the integrity of our whole tax system could be threatened," is headlined "A New U.S. Study on Tax Evasion Is Another Reason To Shout: I'm Mad As Hell And I'm Not Going To Take It Anymore."

Something is going on here. What it does not seem to be is the "tax rebellion" of the amateur constitutional lawyers. What it does seem to be is highly successful and most irritating to the State, its Establishment, and their defenders.

What The "Underground Economy" Is

"Underground Economy" conjures up a vision of some subsociety internal to the general society at large, with consciousness, structured organization, and a subculture of customs, traditions, and perhaps even art and literature. The picture of the underground shopping center in J. Neil Schulman's Alongside Night (Crown, 1979) would fit. But that's set in 2001 — speculative fiction — and no one claims such a subsociety exists today. Furthermore, Schulman's talking about the Counter-Economy, something containing a lot more than tax evasion. So what is the current "Underground Economy" and what is its relation to the Counter-Economy, if any?

The U.S. News & World Report gives the broadest definition of the above sources and the most examples: "In brief, the underground economy involves all the economic activity carried on every day that, for a variety of reasons, escapes tabulation by the nation's official economic pulse takers — from moonlighting and roadside fruit-stands sales to high-level corporate chicanery and multimillion-dollar skimming operations at gambling casinos." So far, it is broad enough to encompass the Counter-Economy. But then, U.S. News narrows it: "This 'work force' is dominated by the self-employed — from lawyers, doctors, and accountants to shopkeepers and tradesmen — and by the working poor. But it includes many from other slices of society, too —
those who, among other things, pad tax deductions or underreport interest, dividend, rental, or royalty income."

Counter-Economics includes everyone. (See later chapters for a proof.) That is, a countereconomic activity is any human action that takes place without the approval of the State. And since laws cover almost every human endeavour, often prohibiting both the action and its corresponding inaction, everyone to at least some small degree must bend or break laws simply to exist.

U.S. News sees considerably fewer people in its "Underground Economy." "In ways small and large, 15 to 20 million Americans probably are involved, says Allen R. Voss, who supervised a study of the problem by the General Accounting Office. Of these, as many as 4.5 million derive all their support from subterranean income, according to Peter M. Gutmann, an economics professor at City University of New York." In short, the "Underground Economy" is the most hard-core committed sector of the tax-law breakers of the Counter-Economy.

Who are the taxless? Several examples, from housecleaning widows to housewife tailors to roadside vegetable-vending farmers are given. This one may be archetypical: "A struggling 24year-old actress in New York City holds down three jobs to make ends meet: She works as a bartender, a job that pays her $30 to $35 a day, including tips; helps out at her father's jewelry shop on Saturdays, and appears occasionally in her own cabaret act at a Greenwich Village night spot.

"All her jobs are off the books. Her employers, in other words, don't withhold any taxes from her pay and don't contribute toward Social Security or unemployment insurance as they are required to do. 'I'm completely underground,' she says. 'There are no records of anything I'm doing.'"

She exhibits no guilt or repentance over her failure to account to the State for her action. One wistful note is struck by the housecleaner. "'As I get older,' she says, 'I'm starting to think, maybe I should have had my people pay on Social Security for me. But this way I pay no taxes, no nothing.'"

While the "Underground Economy" concept is heavily weighted toward tax evasion, the interconnectedness with other counter-economic activities such as Social Security evasion, labor regulations avoidance, health and safety inspection noncompliance, and illegal immigration is obvious

The "Underground Economy" as defined by the IRS, et al., at most includes our actress and her employers. But remember, anyone who deals with her and is aware of her illegal activities is an accessory and co-conspirator. Thus, all her friends, relatives, co-workers and probably many of her customers, fellow thespians, and even barflies are involved in the Counter-Economy. This "ripple" effect is characteristic of Counter-Economics; one need not belabor its effect on the majesty and authority of the State, its agents, and bureaucrats, on those even peripherally involved. '

Every non-statist job or enterprise is capable of some degree of counter-economizing. Some industries seem to have a higher affinity for Counter-Economics than others U.S. News delves into those commercial sectors which, to maintain the metaphor, have a tendency to "submerge." Leading the way is that heterogeneous set of employment opportunities known as moonlighting.

"A whole panoply of moonlighters toils away in the underground economy. One such man, a young New York musician earned $7,500 — almost all of it in cash — by giving guitar lessons last year. But he declared none of it on the joint return he filed with his wife. He didn't list the income, he says, partly out of need and partly out of anger. His parents paid high taxes for years, he says, yet he was denied government loans and grants available to others to help with his college expenses because his parents' income was too high." The connection between anti-state resentment and counter-economic motivation is indicative of the implicit libertarianism of Counter-Economics; the fact that it remains unfocused — currently — might well interest libertarian strategists.

"A moonlighter in Indiana works in a machine-tool shop during the week and oversees a private trash-disposal facility on weekends, where he takes in about $100 in unreported income each week." While hard-core counter-economists are more common than expected (e.g. the actress and musician above), most people are partially counter-economic.

"Millions who work at regular jobs but are not subject to withholding taxes — teachers, taxi drivers, door-to-door salespeople, pollsters, insurance agents, and real-estate brokers, among them — are accused by officials of being a major element in the underground economy. Some 47 percent do not report their earnings, the IRS claims." Interestingly, U.S. News fails to mention waitresses and waiters anywhere in their article; a surprising omission considering the size of that Amazon Army (largely female) with largely unreported tips.

How The Counter-Economic Taxless Do It

How does it work? Fundamentally, as the Internal Revenue Service admits in its ironic way, the income tax is based on voluntary compliance. Where the compliance occurs, it obscures over, is in the information about, not the collection of, its plunder. To put it simply and bluntly, you have to turn yourself in (or have someone you trust do it for you) to get taxed. Breaking down the State's access to information about its victims is a general principle of counter-economic mechanics; the other method involves letting them know when they are impotent to act — which does work in certain fields but is hardly "underground."

This then is the real meaning of "underground" in this context — out of "sight" of the eyes of the State's informants and enforcers. How does this work in day-to-day practice?

 Nearly all the examples given use cash — and complicity. Cash is untraceable; in effect, even if the State suspects, as long as they have the present legal system they cannot prove or convict. They need records — and testimony. The complicity is, of course, bought outright with a discount. (In a few rare cases, especially with artists, artisans, and special drug smugglers, complicity may be purchased by the uniqueness of the product; i.e., you can't get it except by underground agreement.)

Another method, however, operates by the obverse method — no cash. Says U.S. News, "Barter transactions are thought to be another sizable source of untaxed income. A Flint, Michigan, attorney was given a $300 antique credenza by a local resident he represented in a child-support matter. The attorney often swaps services with his clients but does not report as income the value of the items he receives. 'I don't feel guilty about what I do,' he says. 'The government is ripping me off.'" Again we see the anti-state resentment justifying illegality — and the ripple effect in this one lawyer's "contamination" of a whole town full of clients with countereconomic complicity.

"Another man, a self-employed commercial illustrator and copywriter in Chicago who is fed up with high taxes, says he does little cash business but a lot of bartering. He writes advertising copy for a liquor store in exchange for alcoholic beverages he needs for entertaining, and does illustrations for an ad agency in return for typographical services. He figures that the bartering accounts for 5 to 10 percent of his business." Underground enterprise — like the overground type — seems limited only by ingenuity. Of course, the "overground economy" is also limited by the State's control and regulations.

Oh, yes, how does this artist feel about his outlaw activities? "'These trades happen so frequently, on a low economic level, that I can't keep track of how often I do it,' he says. Hiding it from the tax collector would have bothered him a couple of years ago. No longer. 'Now I think of it in terms of economic survival. Taxation has become legalized theft.'" He sounds like an ideological libertarian.

Besides these two methods of keeping income "off the books" to keep it from the tax men, another method is to manipulate the books themselves. One group of retirees collect winnings at race tracks for big-time bettors, then turn them over to their backers who avoid high-bracket income levels. Expense accounts can and do absorb all sorts of transactions to be kept off the personal income books. "Skimming" is nearly universal in small storefront businesses, shops, and taxis: keeping a portion of each day's take without recording it. A jeweler interviewed by U.S. News does $10 million worth of business a year, 25 to 30 percent of it in cold cash. "He says he thinks 10 to 20 percent of all the income generated 'on the street' goes unreported." Massive. And he sounds like Ayn Rand: "I started with nothing and built up a business of millions. The government started with billions, and they keep going in debt. They just waste the money."

And finally, one can simply double the books, one for you and one for the State: "A Houston barber keeps two sets of books, one for herself, one for the IRS. Most business is in cash; she pockets about a third of it, or $200 a week, without reporting it."

One last U.S. News example puts it all together. "A California merchant who boasts that he hasn't paid 1 percent of income tax in five years offers this how-to-do-it advice on skimming: 'The most important thing is consistency. If you skim, skim the same amount each year. If you let one year go by without taking anything off and then take 20 percent the next, you're going to get caught.

"'Even an IRS audit doesn't mean the end of the world. You are usually notified in advance. All you have to do is buy some new receipt books and make them fit your figures. As long as the receipts are numbered consecutively, and the figures jibe, you're O.K. In fact, the year I cheated the government was the year I was audited. The upshot was the inspector ended up congratulating me on what fine shape my records were in. Cheating the government is so easy it's pitiful.'"

What Causes The "Underground Economy?"

The Counter-Economy exists because the State exists. Every intervention by the State in the free market dislocates supply from demand. Besides being the coercive curse that libertarians denounce, each intervention creates an economic opportunity for an entrepreneur to figure out how to supply demand that the State prohibits or cheaper than the State allows.

In the special case of the taxless "Underground Economy," every tax is a challenge. Let's take a look at New York City. Says U.S. News: "New York City's black market in bootleg cigarettes, which by some estimates accounts for up to half of all sales of the tobacco product in the city now, could be denying the city and the State 'hundreds of millions of dollars a year' in revenue, says David Durk, assistant commissioner of enforcement for the city's Department of Finance. The reason for the burgeoning bootleg market: The high excise tax, which totals 23 cents a pack."

Unique? Read on. "New York City's relatively high sales tax of 8 percent poses another problem. It is common for merchants to skim 20 percent of it, says economist Gutmann." And only in New York? "A sales-tax expert, John F. Due, an economics professor at the University of Illinois, says that from 3 to 5 percent of total sales taxes due nationwide, or as much as 2 billion a year, escapes collection."

A second U.S. News article, directly following, "Cheating on Taxes — A Worldwide Pursuit," documents similar figures and adjusted for local cultural practices, around the world. Schwarzarbeit in Germany, travail noir in France, "fiddlers" in Britain, and morocho in Argentina are terms coined to deal with black labor and black money. "Italy's underground economy is growing so rapidly that the government now includes it in economic planning." Argentine government officials "estimate that up to 40 percent of all business is involved." Japan, Sweden, and Canada are covered, and "Economists in Thailand throw up their hands when asked to estimate what uncollected taxes are costing the government. 'Who knows?' is the response given most often." We'll look at the International Counter-Economy in detail next chapter.

Should There Be An "Underground Economy?": Critics and Defenders

There is a Counter-Economy, in particular the sector involved with tax evasion, and it's vast. It was "discovered" and named by this author, speaking to radical libertarians, in 1974. Now the "underground" part, at least, has been discovered by others and they do not approve. While leaving the theory and justification to the end as promised, I think I may whet the reader's appetite by previewing the debate between libertarians and the Establishment writers on just the tax question.

Both camps agree that a perfect society would not have a Counter-Economy, or any part thereof. What they disagree on is that the libertarians see the Counter-Economy as that perfect society in embryo struggling to hatch; the opposition sees it as a blight and unsightly tumor on the more-or-less acceptable body politic.

Welfare state defenders and planners don't like it. Says U.S. News: "governmental programs are upset by the underground economy. Because of unregulated jobs and income, the readings of government statisticians — whose numbers can trigger automatic cost-of-living raises or pump billions of dollars of fiscal adrenalin into the economy when unemployment goes up — may be out of phase with what really is happening. Unemployment, for example, actually may be almost a half percentage point lower than the official figures indicate, says an economist who has studied it, and the number of poverty-stricken somewhat fewer." Libertarians would point out that perhaps the Counter-Economy could absorb all the unemployed, especially when the State
breaks down in runaway inflation or catastrophic depression — which result from the State's own controls.

Ernest Conine of the L.A. Times puts it this way: "In a perfect world, all inequalities would disappear. Pending that unlikely day, however, the complaints that all of us have about government hardly add up to a valid excuse for cheating on taxes." Perhaps not, but what does Conine think is wrong with it? "After all, when a house painter or a lawyer reports only half his income, he isn't hurting David Rockefeller, the Pentagon, Jimmy Carter, the U.S. Supreme Court or the big-time tax evader." Why some or all of them should be hurt would be very enlightening, if explained by an editor of the Los Angeles Times. Alas, no: such analysis is given. And, on top of that, Conine is factually wrong, 180° out of whack. Since all those except the "big-time tax evader" live off the State's taxes, there's that much less a pie for them to divide. If all the economy went "underground," all the aforementioned would be bankrupt.

Who is the counter-economist hurting, according to Conine? "He is hurting the guy down the street who works for a straight paycheck and has no way of avoiding taxes, even if he wanted to, and thus must pay both his share of the tax burden and that of the tax cheat as well." Again Conine is wrong; if his economic theory holds, then if everyone avoided taxes but one unlucky stiff, he or she would support the entire tax burden. There is some "elasticity" to tax "supply" but nothing on the order of 20–30% of the economy. The State is simply collecting fewer taxes — period.

Conine blames "tax cheating" for higher taxes and concludes, "Somehow, though, this is a case where too many people instinctively side not with the cops but with the robbers... Most of us seem determined to go right on looking on small-bore tax cheats with bemused tolerance — even playing their game with off-the-books cash payments for services rendered — in blithe disregard of the fact that they are placing their fair share of the tax burden on our shoulders." '

Further in the book, the "guy with the straight paycheck" will find more ways, if he hasn't picked up several already, on how he can join the taxless. One chapter will deal with Brown of Pacific News Service's fear of illegal alien exploitation and lack of security, the large literature already extant on free-market economics answers Sylvia Porter's fears of the collapse of society, and the collapse of the State in society, that is, how the Counter-Economy can expand to overwhelm the State's economy and create a free society, and sell it to an oppressed, angry people already fighting back to the limits of their understanding, will be dealt with in the final chapter of the book.

What a fair share of the tax burden, if any, is takes us into the theory, which is being put off. Suffice it to say here that if Conine believes a relatively free society of people have the right to choose their own taxation level, with or without representation, then he should welcome those who are effectively making that choice. But it's not only the relatively free people in the United States who are able to make that choice via Counter-Economics. Now we shall turn to the rest of the world.

5. International Counter-Economics

Having established the existence of at least the taxless part of the Counter-Economy and at least in this continent, one has two directions to expand the concept — other fields in this continent and Counter-Economics abroad. There is also the combination of the two — the countereconomy across the borders of this continent and those of others.

In a free market, there are no borders. There are geography, space to be crossed with goods and information, and obstacles to be overcome all affecting the price. When the State imposes imaginary boundaries and real enforcers such as customs inspectors, immigration officers, and treasury agents — not to mention armies and navies — the market splits. The white market sees obstacles; the black market sees opportunities. To counter-economists, a border is just another obstacle to moving goods and services to be dealt with efficiently and competitively.

Some of the goods smuggled include people, money, and things — the last known as contraband and can be anything from jeans to cocaine. Another field of border-avoiding commerce is transporting information. That can range from "pirate broadcasting" to industrial and political espionage. There is even a tactic of moving legally acceptable goods across borders to take advantage of different tax breaks and export incentives.

This may be the best time to point out that there are places with virtually no counter-economy (though counter-economists from other areas may be operating here only): space, the high seas, and the free ports. The rapid militarization and nationalization of the first two is generating Counter-Economics and will be covered later. The third category describes areas where the States of the world have contracts (treaty) to refrain from control — though that is revocable at any time, as Danzig and Tangiers found out. Even Hong Kong and Singapore were briefly occupied during World War II. One can draw what lessons one wishes from these places which have no economic intervention and no counter-economy, and standards of living far higher than their surroundings.

Almost every major country, by the way, has free-trade zones at airports and seaports to allow transfer of goods from international carrier to international carrier. New York City has one on Staten Island. Prominent pedophiliac Roman Polanski, subject to arrest on sight in the United States, landed at Los Angeles International and took off again en route from France to Tahiti. He was not molested, though he wisely remained in the plane throughout. Such areas of free trade are hardly the result of State benevolence or laxity; should a State eliminate such boons to trade, another State in the "international anarchy" will offer the service and increase the share of business.

What about the "underground economy" of tax evasion? Does that exist abroad? In many places, taxation is worse than in the United States, so expecting the more Counter-Economics the more the intervention, we should find plenty.

The International "Underground Economy"

The term Schwarzarbeit in West Germany and travail noir in France both mean "black labor." "Whatever this hidden market is called, in Europe it means that workers evade income tax, social security, and often other taxes by failing to report their full earnings to the government. Employers dodge social-welfare taxes, and, in some countries, value-added levies. They also avoid paying higher wages to regular employees for overtime." How many are involved? "Experts at the International Labor Office in Geneva estimate that in Europe 5 percent or more of the total labor force may be involved in the hidden economies. That means 7 to 8 million workers!"[1]

Outside of the Warsaw Pact, the most socialist — statist — country is usually considered to be Sweden. "Sweden, the most heavily taxed nation in Europe, has a hidden economy that is estimated to total at least 10 percent of the national output — and to cost the government taxes amounting to 15 percent of the budget." Labor barter seems to be the main method, and the Swedish State is trying mightily to suppress counter-economic labor "and tighten its tax controls, already among the toughest in Europe. But authorities seem to be fighting a losing battle..."[2]

"Italy's underground economy is growing so rapidly that the government now includes it in economic planning. Official estimates put income from hidden labor at around 10 percent of the gross national product — or about 24 billion dollars — in 1978. But a recent study said it is much greater, as high as 43 billion dollars in 1979."

Counter-economic labor marketing benefits both employer and employee, cutting across class lines even in class-obsessed Europe. Why? The black laborers of Italy "usually receive lower wages, put in longer hours and have no social-security or other fringe benefits. But they pay no taxes."[3] Those who wish to argue that labor wants to avoid risk and trusts the government to protect it from exploiting entrepreneurs, will have to deal with this inconvenient existence: "More than six million workers, one-third of Italy's labor force. are secretly employed." And for the Italian employers, Counter-Economics "lowers their labor costs, gives them a flexible work force and enables them to require employees to work overtime when needed."[4]

Has only Italian labor acquired counter-economic consciousness? "The owner of a clothing factory — staffed with illegal workers — may sell his product to a middleman. The middleman, operating from a delivery van, sells to a retailer. The retailer does not register the purchase and thus can sell at a discount because he has not paid the value-added tax."[5] Note how layers of economic activity form between the initial producer and the final consumer and these layers form counter-economic steps in the "capital pyramid."[6] No step of production seems safe — for the statist.

"Yet, why is it that you seldom hear a peep about deregulation under the blue skies of the sunny Mediterranean? ... The realization dawns first on the autostrada. On roads marked 100 km/h, the only vehicle observing the speed limit is a lone Morris Minor with British licence plates and a flat tire. On the zebra pedestrian crossings in the piazzas you can see bicycles, motor scooters and oxcarts — but no pedestrians. They are darting in and out of the lanes marked 'Buses Only,' where even the oldest Italians do not remember ever having seen a bus. Currency regulations are strict but stores or toll booths accept anything from dollars to Swiss francs and then give you change in gaily wrapped bubble gum to compensate for a shortage in minted coin. A doorman at the Clritti

Palace Hotel in Venice explains why water taxis are charging three times the official tariff. He proudly points to the computerized income tax forms the government in Rome sends everybody. 'The Americans showed our government how to do it,' he says."

Our observer, Ms. Amiel, sees the answer quite counter- economically. "Suddenly the coin, or perhaps the bubble gum, drops. Of course there is little talk about deregulation in Italy. Why fight the paper tiger? The marvelous Mediterranean spirit, the Italian genius, the wise, vital flow of brio, has solved the problem without it. The Italians have cut the Gordian knot.

"They can have all the rules and regulations in the world; they will simply not observe them. The Italians have raised civil disobedience to a fine, subtle art. They have made regulations what most of them deserve to be — the dead letters of someone else's desire."[7]

France has less tax oppression and the travail noir is estimated at — only — 800,000 workers and five billion dollars, though that is undoubtedly an underestimate. "Most hidden work is in plumbing, painting, roofing, electrical installation, and other home repairs. But dressmaking, auto and truck repairs, hairdressing, and carpentry are also popular." So far no one had checked out data processing there.

The ranks of the government itself are not immune. "Even such civil servants as policemen moonlight at night or on weekends." More on that in a bit, How about welfare cases? "Some persons who draw high unemployment benefits prefer full-time underground jobs to working legally."[8]

Union statism adds incentive to West German Counter-Economics. where lower taxes might otherwise depress motivation. (Artificially high wage rates create a barrier to entry leaving jobs undone.) Schwarzarbeiters combat the artificially high wage rates. "Plumbers and bricklayers, who charge $17 to $25 an hour if employed openly through a contractor, can be hired secretly for half that price."[9] It's impossible to assign market value without recording transactions, but German officials estimate twenty-five billion dollars of untaxed work a year costing their State four billion in taxes — which assumes it would even have been performed if taxed.

Insidiously and erroneously, "a state labor ministry says 230,000 West Germans could find work if Schwarzarbeit were eliminated." The millions of black workers who would be unemployed are of no consequence to the labor ministry.[10]

Fines of $380,000 were imposed with one worker in Stuttgart fined $5,000 and taxed $112,000 for earning $250,000 in seven years. "But fines do not seem to help."[11]

"In Great Britain these underground workers are called 'fiddlers.' It is estimated that one of every eight Britons earns a minimum of $2,200 a year by moonlighting and does not pay a penny of tax on the unofficial income. By one reckoning, the black economy accounts for close to 8% of Britain's gross national product."[12] Those who fear for the stifling of British incentive under social democracy may take heart. The British are counter-economizing with the same techniques as the American and European, but there are a few unique cases.

"One fiddle that is hard to bring under control is taking place on the oil rigs in the North Sea. Many British companies and subsidiaries of foreign firms cooperate with the government's payas-you earn plan and deduct taxes from employees' pay, But some drillers refuse to do so... up to now, about 8,000 workers have paid no taxes on earnings of about 90 million dollars."[13]

Earlier, cross-border Counter-Economics for purposes of tax evasion was mentioned. Some spectacular cases of Swedish movie stars and English rock stars are well known. Here's the testimony of a lumpenbourgeoisie: "If I worked at home, I might make as much as $400 a week, out of which I'd have to pay rent, buy food — and pay taxes, But, doing the same work in Germany or Holland, I get $700 a week plus meals and a place to live. I take my money in cash and don't pay taxes to anybody."[14]

On to the Third World: Argentina calls it black money — morocho — that is tax free, and estimates 40% of all business is involved.[15] "The head of a construction company sums up the situation this way: 'You won't have a hammer swinging anywhere in this country unless you are prepared to pay black money.'" And in the higher classes, "A banker in Buenos Aires reports: 'The apartment next to ours was sold a few weeks ago for $360,000 — all in cash and all black money. There were no taxes, no real estate commission, no anything except $360,000 in cash.'"[16]

While tax evasion is relatively minor in Japan (so far), Counter-Economics enters where the monopolist State education system creates artificial "barriers to entry" (the economist term which one will be seeing a lot of here). To enter the more prestigious universities requires the payment of "backdoor" admission fees. "Parents have paid the yen equivalent of from $4,600 to $460,000 to school officials in order to get their children into their chosen university."[17]

Thailand, near the black-market haven of Burma, makes up for Japan's law-abiding. "The taxpolicy division of the Finance Ministry estimates that less than 10% of the country's 19-millionmember labor force files tax returns."[18] That's 90% who do not file tax returns. Somebody must be watching those 10% like hawks. Just to make sure the incentive is to play and not fink, "an auto salesman offers a prospective customer a 'friendship price' of from 10 to 30 percent off the list price if the buyer pays in cash and agrees to forget any paper work that could be used by tax collectors to trace the sale."[19]

Returning to Italy for a bit, one finds a counter-economic effect even more threatening to the State. It seems the majority of that six million (1979 estimate[20]) or two to four million (1977 estimate[21]) are the government workers themselves! Working from 8 A.M. to 1:30 P.M., the Roman bureaucrats are well positioned for afternoon second jobs.[22]

"'Yes, I know I'm taking up a job someone else needs,' says a bureaucrat in the Italian Finance Ministry who supplements his $400 a month government salary by working in a real estate office in the afternoons and by skipping his government job in the mornings if a big deal comes up. 'But I've got to look out for my wife and three children.'"[23]

The rise of British CB and smuggling of various goods such as drugs, guns, and people will be taken up in their appropriate chapters. Still, remember that the business generated is tax-free: "The Coast Guard estimates that six to eight

88

billion dollars in illicit weed was successfully smuggled by ship into the U.S. last year."[24]

That's just one product and one method of shipping. And yet, "you ain't seen nothing yet." Let us turn now to the Eastern bloc, the Warsaw Pact and other nations laboring under Marxism, Leninism, and variants thereof.

Counter-Economics Under Communism

Argentina, ruled mostly by a military dictatorship, seems to have a thriving counter-economy as we have seen. Is there a substantive difference between "authoritarian" regimes of right-wing statism and "totalitarian" regimes of left-wing statism — at least in this regard? A drug haven like Colombia or Bolivia, riddled with corruption, may have a booming counter-economy but what about Third World countries cleaned up and reformed by Marxist-Leninist governments? Perhaps the most important question in this area is, can the power of the State get so great that the counter-economy, rather than growing in response, gets crushed?

Viet Nam could answer all these questions. After all, were there not dire predictions of catastrophe, nay, apocalypse, when the free-enterprise Americans were driven out by the
Communist North Vietnamese? Would anyone making the distinction between authoritarian and totalitarian states deny post-1973 Viet Nam is the latter? Is not Viet Nam both "Third World" and "Second World?"

Back in July of 1976, this author noticed a report on Viet Nam and wrote it up as follows; it is printed in its entirety.

The "corruption" which so tainted the Thieu-Ky regime and the U. S. sergeants has infected the Lao Dong (Communist Party) cadre in "liberated" Saigon, according to reporter Patrice de Beer in a two-part article in the weekly English edition of Le Monde, the famous French daily.

"Not a dollar has dropped into Saigon's empty coffers since April 30, 1973, not a bag of American rice has come to alleviate the crop shortfalls," reports Beer. Elsewhere, he describes the scene in the present Saigon.

"Yet the city streets are crowded with cars and motorized bikes. Swarms of prostitutes ply their trade in the old To Do street, and the thieves' market offers piles of stereo sets, fans, and other American goods brought out from heaven knows where. I was even held up for a quarter of an hour in a traffic jam while trying to drive out of the city."

Beer goes on to describe the problem of the new society "Some members of the new ruling class (a very tiny fraction, I was assured, but quite conspicuous) are following in the footsteps of their predecessors, providing the prostitutes with a new clientele, especially in the centrally situated Miramar Hotel, occupied by cadres. Waiters in the posh restaurants complain that the 'bodoi' (soldiers of the People's Army) are not good customers because they don't have any money. 'But the "canbos" (cadres) are good customers. They are rich and give fat tips.'"

Now Beer describes what a libertarian would call a full-blown counter-economy: "Exit visas are rumoured to be going for hundreds of dollars, gasoline intended for arms and government use finds its way into the black market, and civil servants or persons posing as civil servants are alleged to solicit bribes from families for freeing a husband or brother sent to a re-education center. Some of the leaders live in requisitioned villas, and have cars, buy furniture, television sets, and let themselves be corrupted by the old bourgeoisie, which knows in the long run its fate is sealed, and is not therefore inclined to be optimistic. Those who have decided to stay are spending everything they have. This accounts for the rush on expensive restaurants and a frenzied buying spree, which is fueling an inflationary flare-up."

Students of Austrian economics will smile at Patrice de Beer's reversal of cause and effect on his inflation analysis, and note the classic description of a "flight into real goods."

Beer goes on to report the vicious gossip about the "bodoi" and "canbos", the investigation by the Lao Dong of corruptions, the hostility between Northerners and Southerners.

"As for the Northerners, they are dazed at the sight of the South's apparent prosperity, for they have been told their compatriots were short of everything.

"The demobilisation has just begun and a number of 'bodoi' have been assigned jobs in the economy. They are still being asked to make sacrifices to help their 'brothers in the South,' though in their eyes the South Vietnamese don't seem so badly off."

Being a Communist country, Viet Nam naturally has a Five-Year Plan. But it sounds strangely like something from Ford or Carter: "The south's so called policy of 'five economic sectors' — state, co-operative, mixed, capitalist, and private — should continue for some time more to come. As Nguyen Huu Tho pointed out, the state must 'use capitalism's qualities and curb its negative tendencies.' ... He added it was necessary to be 'flexible, very realistic, and be able at times to fall back a little.' Principles couldn't be bent any further in a situation where officially the country is headed towards a socialist type of economy. It ought to be mentioned that even in the North there is a lively private sector nicknamed the 'under-the-counter sector.'"[25]

That was 1976. Surely, that was too close to the end of the war with the United States. Things must have changed, say, four years later?

"The economy is strictly black market. Privately run shops remain open, but they are musty places full of cheap, imitation lacquer dishes and mind-numbing political treatises, all at outrageous prices.

"There also are government shops where civil servants and government enterprise employees buy their monthly food rations.

"A laborer is entitled to 13 kilograms of rice a month — just under one pound a day — and the scale goes downward to the office clerk, who is allotted less than one-quarter pound a day

"There is rarely enough rice to go around. There also are limp vegetables and the occasional piece of pork or beef." A miserable scene is observed after seven years of communism, as predicted... except for one thing.

"The black market is called Cho Troi or 'sky market' because goods are displayed outdoors. Here, in the side streets and the central marketplace with its satellites throughout the city, is the collective economy of Ho Chi Minh City.

"Prices are fearsome, but the market is the only place such exotic items as razor blades, soap that makes suds, fresh food, tape cassettes, and decent cloth are available.

"Gasoline at more than $15 a gallon may be the most expensive in the world. That tiny razor blade is $5 and the highly prized Lux brand American toilet soap $11.

"In a place where official salaries average less than $100 a month, such luxuries as electricity and a telephone have become virtual objects of curiosity.

"The black market thrives on the official 'intershop,' which is open to all foreigners and accepts major currencies of the world — but not the Vietnamese dong, worth 43 cents at the official rate."[26]

Perhaps seven years after the Revolution is not enough. How about the People's Republic of China, twenty-one years after its Revolution? "In a dragnet of Shanghai, China's largest metropolis, the police have arrested nearly 200 black marketeers in recent weeks and confiscated valuables ranging from television sets and tape cassettes to marriage manuals and 'pornographic materials,' the Shanghai newspaper Wen Hui Bao reported."[27]

How does one conduct Counter-Economics in such incredibly crowded conditions? "Privacy is nonexistent here; so even an illicit business must be conducted in the open, but the black marketeers are more subtle than most. On bustling Zhongshan Road the other day, a huge crowd of youths surrounded an older man who was playing a brand new Sanyo tape recorder. They listened awhile, then disappeared into a side street cafe. One young man returned, the tape recorder tucked under his arm, It had obviously changed hands in the cafe.

"Another favorite device is for people hawking sunglasses from abroad to keep the foreign sticker on one lens, attesting to the place of origin. Foreign sunglasses, the latest status symbol for China's young, sell on the black market at tremendous markups, typically $25 for a pair that costs $5 in Hong Kong."[28]

The Chinese Counter-Economy is limited neither in scope nor in geography. "High-quality consumers goods, available here only in small quantities and in government control, account for most of the illicit trade, but there are exotic items, too. Black marketeers have been nabbed here for selling a Chinese-language sex manual, A Guide to a Happy Marriage. And heroin is smuggled into Guangdong province from Hong Kong.

"Black market activities thrive in this pace-setting city, where 11.6 million people seem a bit more prosperous and decidedly more stylish than most Chinese, but the more staid places are not immune.

"In a so-far unsuccessful drive to stop illegal trading in Beijing, perhaps China's most tightly controlled city, capital police have repeatedly raided the black market on Dongdon Street. Yet on many Sunday afternoons, young speculators still gather in the same spot, less than a mile from the Public Security Ministry, to swap goods."[29]

Nevertheless, all regions of China are not equal, counter- economically. (All regions of, say, the U.S., are not equal economically, either.) The areas bordering on "capitalist" countries seem, naturally enough, to have a better counter-economy, at least in terms of availability of goods. "Because it lies next door to the British colony of Hong Kong, Guangdong province in South China appears to be the entry point for black market goods. It also boasts what Chinese sources believe to be China's largest black market, in Fatshan, a 20-minute bus ride outside Guangzhou.

"Fatshan is so well-stacked with watches, radios, tape recorders, calculators, television sets, and other luxuries that it is a magnet for people from all over China.

"Even official purchasing agents from rural communes, under orders to buy scarce goods for collective use, turn to Fatshan when supplies at the government stores are depleted."[30]

One would probably, at this point, expect the area close to the Republic of China on Taiwan to be riddled with marketeering. "Quanzhou, which lies on the coast of Fujian province opposite the Nationalist-held island of Taiwan, is dotted with vendors selling Dunhill, Viceroy, and other Western cigarettes for 65 cents to $1.30 a pack. Squatting on the dusty roads, they display their wares openly, but fold up shop and hurry off when approached by cameras.

"Other sidewalk stalls display tapes recorded by Teresa Teng, a Taiwan torch singer whose romantic ballads are hits throughout China though she has never set foot on the mainland. Like the other merchandise, the tapes were smuggled in from Hong Kong, one vendor acknowledged."[31]

Smuggling will be covered in a chapter coming soon but there is one thing we ought to check on. After all, there is far more repression of it by the anti-market Communists than the freedomloving Nationalists, right? "Although arrests have been made on both sides, the Nationalists appear to be far more concerned than the Beijing government about stopping the trade. A special investigation force was organized last month in Taipei to probe the smuggling rings, a government spokesman said, and further arrests are anticipated. Under Taiwan's strict martial law trading with 'the enemy,' the Communists, is a traitorous act punishable by long prison sentences."[32]

If there is any place which might have the free market utterly stamped out, it would have to be Cambodia, after Pol Pot and the additional devastations of the war driving him out.

"The black market stretches from Bangkok, Thailand's capital, to Ho Chi Minh City, formerly Saigon, in southern Vietnam. Its hub is this dirty town of war-gutted houses and tin-roofed shacks swollen by transients from almost every province in the country.

"Sisophon is about 30 miles from the frontier, where Thai merchants have set up open air supermarkets to which the Cambodians flock despite occasional robbers and fighting en route and guerrillas who take a cut of the trade."[33]

Can nothing stop the Counter-Economy from its activity? Nope. "It all starts with gold exchanged at the border for Thai currency, the baht. The Cambodian trafficker uses the baht to make his purchases, which are then resold here, usually for gold again. But this is only the small loop of a seemingly haphazard, but in fact highly effective, distribution system.

"Armies of bicyclists, averaging 30 miles a day, set out from here along the country's major roads, especially routes 5 and 6 to Phnom Penh, the capital. Bulging sacks and boxes are lashed to the bicycle seats, and bolts of cloth sometimes dangle and flap behind as the dealer pushes the bike along.

"Some travel between their homes and the border; others drop off their goods at the 'free markets' which thrive in almost all the towns. Bike repair shops and refreshment stands dot the roadsides for benefit of the traders who also move on foot, ox-carts, motorcycles, military and civilian trucks, and the train from Phnom Penh to Battambang, 25 miles east of the frontier."[34]

We all know of the lack of production in Democratic Kampuchea… or is it the government's lack rather than the people of Cambodia? "The 14-month-old government has been able to give little else but rice from foreign donors to the general population, and has difficulties distributing it. So most, including most government officials, must shop on the free market where medicines, watches, clothes, cigarettes, and even Japanese-made radio-cassette players and motorcycles are available."[35]

No starvation in Phnom Penh, evacuated by Pol Pot and reduced to basic, primitive communism? "At Phnom Penh's bustling old market one can, thanks to unbridled free enterprise, sit down to a good roast duck and vegetables, canned

Australian or Japanese beer, and international-aid rice that has seeped into the system."[36]

Of course there was privation in Cambodia and many people died. But the Counter-Economy survived and burgeoned. And the Counter-Economy, let one never forget. is human action — that is, humans acting. Some in Cambodia retain their incentive and produce against the worst threats a government can issue and in the face of all the examples of the death threats carried out. They are those greedy, heartless, cowardly, profit-gouging, couldn't-care-for-their-fellow-man speculative enterprisers — who, by all accounts, alone keep Cambodia from total starvation imposed by the people-loving Communists of Pol Pot and his equally Communist opponent, Heng Samrin.

Perhaps the final irony is that not only does right-wing Thailand's market supply the Cambodian Counter-Economy, but also Samrin's ally's Counter-Economy — Viet Nam itself! "Although most of the trade is with Thailand, there is also a sizeable two-way commerce with Viet Nam. Consumer goods such as tea, soap, fruit, and bicycle parts make their way to Cambodia. But the Vietnamese, sometimes coming by truck to deliver aid or supplies for their forces, also haul back Thai goods which they purchase from the Cambodians with gold."[37]

Counter-Economics In The Second World

There's one last possibility one must exclude before concluding that the Counter-Economy cannot be suppressed but rather will thrive under even greater statism. Perhaps all Asiatic or South American (Cuban) Communist states are too new, too Oriental (by which is usually meant prone to corruption) or Latin, or just too weak to stand up to the mighty wealth of world capitalism. If anywhere answers these objections, it is the nations of the Warsaw Pact — the Eastern bloc, where the Union of Soviet Socialist Republics holds far more sway in the name of Marx and Lenin than does capitalist NATO and its running-dog lackeys.

Poland is considered anomalous because of the rise of Solidarity, so it will be accepted as a poor example for our proof. Solidarity's rise, however, must then be credited to the counter-economic case since it organized and struck in defiance of all Polish laws. In fact, most unions even in the United States began counter-economically. (What they turned into and why is left for later.)

In 1976, Poland experienced a mass upheaval which subsided until Solidarity's rise. "The prime minister of Poland ordered price increases of staples, food, clothes, etc., in the state-owned stores. Immediately, demonstrations of consumers hit the streets, similar to those which toppled First Secretary Gomulka and brought in present dictator Edward Gierek. Within 24 hours, Gierek's prime minister suspended his own orders.

"One factor not mentioned in most press coverage was that these same goods were available to some extent in a number of private stores allowed and in the widespread black market. The Guardian noted that the counter-economic price was higher than the state price even after the official price increase, yet business is brisk."[38]

So how free is the stable Eastern bloc from Counter-Economics? "Romanians, unlike Poles, are not officially allowed to possess foreign currency, but this does not stop the inevitable money changers from accosting foreigners on the streets. The black market rate has rocketed since the Polish crisis began and is now five times the official rate, or more, the most coveted currency in Romania is a packet of foreign cigarettes (preferably Kents). In a practice that constitutes the thin edge of the wedge of bribery and corruption — an integral part of East European life — a packet of cigarettes is slipped to the head waiter, and food and drink, which were off the menu five minutes before, miraculously reappear. A foreign businessman, who lives in Romania but drives a foreign-registered car, is stopped by the police. A packet of cigarettes, and documents that were suspect a moment before are suddenly in order. Those packets of cigarettes change hands again for under-the-counter food supplies for quality clothing, for house repairs. And they oil the wheels of bureaucracy."[39]

Actually, much of the Counter-Economy of the East works like that of Western Europe described earlier: "The system involves second and third jobs, many performed for Western currency, which in turn may be used to buy luxuries. In Hungary, Poland, and Czechoslovakia, the second economy has grown so dominant that many workers have come to devote more of their time and energy to that sector than to their regular jobs.

"Construction workers in Czechoslovakia and Hungary are rarely found on their regular jobs past the noontime lunch break. They are off on their second or third jobs."[40]

Want to buy a car in Hungary but the State says no? "A housekeeper in Budapest hotel told how, despite recent police crackdowns, she was still able to order a new-model Soviet-built Lada automobile from a local underground supplier, delivery in one month, for a price 50 percent higher than the official price, cash in full on delivery.

"Her supplier, to whom she cautiously introduced a Western correspondent, said that the system operated with the connivance of official dealers. They find customers who have been on a waiting list for two or three years, but who are willing, for a price, to give up their new car and begin the wait again."[41]

Some Eastern counter-economists seem to have it better than "Free World" workers, beating inflation. "When consumer prices rose 50 percent or more in Hungary this summer, a carpenter in a tractor factory said he could easily cope. His salary went up less than 10 percent, but his fees for fine cabinet work he produces nights and weekends doubled."[42]

Hungarians have their entrepreneurial laborers, their travail noir and schwarzarbeiters. "Then there are the 'sparrows,' a term used in Hungary for the highly skilled workers who flit from job to job, increasing their wages by steady increments as demand shifts from one enterprise to another."[43]

And in competitive education, depending on the Counter-Economy, the Easterners may well be ahead of the West. "In Poland it has taken on a new dimension, with 'flying high schools' spreading forbidden subjects. These range from the rule of terror by Poland's Stalinist-era leader, Boleslaw Bierat, to the economics of Milton Friedman and Paul A. Samuelson."[44] As always, we ask how it works.

"While such lectures may reach only a few thousand of Poland's 100,000 or more university students, the influence of these ideas is much wider. Several young men and women were taping a lecture by an underground historian, Adam Michnik, held at a blacked-out suburban Warsaw apartment.

"'My roommates are too scared to come,' one of them said. 'But they want to hear it, so I tape it and they listen later.'"[45]

Why does and how can Mother Russia allow this rampant free enterprise in her closely-guarded satellites? Or has the Counter-Economy beached the innermost Iron Curtain as well? That story deserves a chapter unto itself.

Footnotes:

1. The underground economy: How 20 million Americans cheat Uncle Sam out of billions in taxes. (1979, October 22). U.S. News & World Report, p. 53.
2. Ibid.
3. Ibid.
4. Ibid.
5. Ibid.
6. Böhm-Bawerk, E. V. (1890) Capital and Interest. New York: Macmillan
7. Amiel, B. (1981, July 13). The subtle art of disobedience. Macleans 94(28), p. 52.
8. U.S. News & World Report, op. cit., p. 53.
9. Ibid.
10. Ibid., p. 54.
11. Ibid.
12. Ibid.
13. Ibid.
14. Ibid.
15. Ibid.
16. Ibid.
17. Ibid.
18. Ibid.
19. Ibid.
20. Ibid.

21. Hoagland, J. (1977, September 18). European tide of "black labour." Manchester Guardian Weekly, Washington Post section.

22. Ibid.

23. Ibid.

24. The marijuana smuggling war is heating up on the high seas. (1981, January 5). Zodiac News Service.

25. Counter-economy in Viet Nam thrives. (1978, August 1). New Libertarian Weekly 3(34), pp. 1, 4.

26. Los Angeles Times, Wednesday, July 23, 1980, Part IA, page 5.

27. Mathews, L. (1980, June 7). Black marketeers, smugglers move in as China opens trade door to the world. Los Angeles Times, Part I, 6-7. (The headline is inaccurate as the article proves that there is a black market, not that it moved in from anywhere.)

28. Ibid.

29. Ibid.

30. Ibid.

31. Ibid.

32. Mathews, L. (n.d., c. 1980) China, Taiwan crack down on smugglers. Los Angeles Times.

33. Gray, D. D. (1980, April 13). Black market net funnels consumer goods to Cambodia. Santa Ana Register, p. D15.

34. Ibid.

35. Ibid.

36. Ibid.

37. Ibid.

38. Free market cracks red regimes. (1976, July 25). New Libertarian Weekly 3(33), p. 1. 39. Masterman, S., and Koene, A. (1981, August 24). A nation embarked on a perilous ride: Eerily reminiscent of Poland, growing tension threatens the oppressive Ceausescu regime. Macleans 94(34), p. 11.

40. Second society grows in Europe. (1979, November 2). New York Times.

41. Ibid.

42. Ibid.

43. Ibid.

44. Ibid.

45. Ibid

3. Soviet Counter–Economics

A major premise of counter-economic theory is this: the more government intervention in the economy, the larger the Counter-Economy. Indeed, as we have moved from the "limited governments" of North America to the "mixed economies" of the rest of the world, counter-economic activity has certainly not receded. Counter-Economics, moreover, predicts that totalitarian states should conduct nearly all economic activity — in fact, all non-political and even much political human action — outside the area sanctioned by the State. So a positive test of our theory would be to check out a totalitarian State in some detail and observe the degree of counter-economic activity.

A minor qualification is in order, though we shall see it is scarcely needed for our test. The economic theory which forms the most basic level of our understanding predicts that no state can achieve totalitarian control. In fact, Counter-Economics was discovered by this author when I followed that idea to further conclusions. But all the so-called totalitarian states — Third Reich, Soviet Russia, People's Republic of China, even Cambodia — actually allowed and continue to allow some "private" property and some freedom of trade.

Nonetheless, most observers will grant there is considerably more state intervention in, say, the Union of Soviet Socialist Republics than in the United States. Therefore, there should be more Counter-Economics, as well.

Let this point be belabored a little more. American conservatism predicts that entrepreneurialism should be almost snuffed out under a totalitarian communist state, except for a few Bible-smugglers. Liberalism and democratic socialism might predict some resistance to communism but that it would take the form of intellectual dissenters and underground unions surfacing into "Charter 77" and "Solidarity" organizations. Even what passes for libertarianism these days predicts less, rather than more, "free market" activity in endarkened U.S.S.R. than in relatively enlightened U.S.A. So if Counter-Economics contradicts all these ideologies' predictions — and it does — one has a quick scientific decision in respect to their respective validity.

What does reality say? We've seen a strong indication in our last chapter looking at Eastern Europe, China, and Indo-China, but we need a much longer, more detailed look at one such country. And if the Counter-Economy is booming in the Soviet Union, the "hardest case" for our theory, then where are the millionaires? Save for a corrupt Commissar or two — even the Communist Party line will allow for such imperfection — who has heard of Russian capitalist pig millionaires in the 1980s?

Consider this: "A few weeks ago the Manchester Guardian Weekly reported that several counter-economic millionaires were arrested in their Black Sea resorts and dachas. Nearly all the government officials in Armenia were also pulled in and broken by the Communist Party and denounced by the press. The Armenian bureaucrats had been involved in a major black and grey market 'ring.' (Armenia had somewhat looser regulations and more private ownership allowed than in Russia.)"[1]

Armenia, it may be argued, is not Russia proper, though a "Soviet Socialist Republic." Then again, the Armenian counter-economists were arrested. How about neighbouring Georgia?

"The parallel market represents a huge economic structure, simultaneously independent from and associated with, the official Soviet economy. This private sector penetrates every segment of Soviet society. People active in the parallel market vary, from petty speculators selling fashionable clothes to people of real influence and wealth, such as the famous Georgian underground capitalist Laziashvily, whose connections include quite a few top officials."[2]

What about Russia itself? "I particularly recall one such spirited client, Abram Aizenberg — a massive man whose every movement expressed self-assurance. He was about 70, and he owned two factories manufacturing hosiery and underwear that brought him an annual income of several hundred thousand rubles. Over the years he had amassed capital that the investigators estimated at three million rubles."[3]

"After World War II, the three Glazenberg brothers were demobilized, returned to Moscow, and soon realized that they could not bank on their being veterans to help them find a good job; they were Jews — banned from all prominent posts in the party and state apparatus. Even Jewish engineers had a hard time finding employment in industry." While some may question the ethnic purity of the entrepreneurs in question, this is Moscow our Russian reporter is talking about.

"The Glazenberg brothers went into underground business. Upon discharge from the army they each received the large sum awarded to demobilized officers — about 5,000 in today's rubles — and acquired a single workshop in a factory to produce artificial-leather shopping bags.

"They turned out to be talented businessmen, and in a few years their company owned at least ten factories manufacturing artificial leather, artificial-leather goods, and all sorts of synthetic fiber products."

Of course, knowledge of their activities comes from their public exposure, arrest and prosecution. "A firm operating on such a large scale could not escape the notice of the Moscow DCMSP (Department for Combatting Misappropriation of Socialist Property, the arm of the Soviet police charged with fighting economic crimes). Indeed, the DCMSP with its well developed network of secret informers, kept a special dossier on the Glazenbergs' company."[4]

How did these Russian entrepreneurs last so long as to get successful in the first place? "For some while, this in no way inhibited the busy entrepreneurs — for they were paying off the top people in the DCMSP, offering a monthly balm of between 5,000 and 10,000 rubles." And how did they get caught? "One day, however, a lower DCMSP officer leaked the story to a wellknown journalist at Izvestia, who began sifting through the material on the brothers' company. In these circumstances the DCMSP chiefs were powerless to save the Glazenbergs — beyond warning them immediately of the danger impending, so they might have time to secrete their money and valuables."

So how did the ruthless, inhuman, infamous, Soviet secret police deal with these bloated capitalists? "Buffeted by the contrary pressures, a top DCMSP official decided in Soviet Solomonic style that 1.) the incriminating dossier would disappear from the DCMSP files and 2.) the youngest Glazenberg brother, Lazar, would have to be sacrificed, at least partly because of his playboy lifestyle reflected in his two dozen suits and the wardrobe of his wife, a ballerina in the Bolshoi theater."

One supposes, at this point, whether the proletarian masses would revile or just ignore this exposed bourgeois. "On the first day of Lazar's trial, the courtroom was packed with curious onlookers, dying to glimpse a millionaire. What they saw was a tall man of about 40 with handsome features and a mane of completely gray hair. Lazar Glazenberg walked, as prisoners are meant to walk, between two escorts, with his hands folded behind his back hobbling along on the artificial leg that replaced the limb he had lost in the war. But he affably greeted friends and relations among the crowd."

Nonetheless, as all have agreed, the U.S.S.R. is a particularly interventionist and repressive society. Our Horatio Algerov was sentenced and shot, no? "Three months later he walked out of the courtroom just as calmly, having heard his sentence: 15 years in strict-regime camps." This is the home of the Stalin purge trials, where the top communist officials — the new Russian aristocracy — are regularly rounded up and shot.

A hardier entrepreneur might have survived and considered himself ahead. Alas, Lazar Glazenberg had "served his country" one limb defending the Motherland. "It is almost impossible for a person with one leg to survive 15 years in such a camp. He died seven years after his trial."[5] Before one reaches for the handkerchief over this typically ironic Russian tragedy, remember the rest of the family got away with their wealth and obviously enough capital to keep going.

So were the Glazenbergs an isolated example? Even if one assumes most are not caught and not reported, there still are plenty who were. That is, there are plenty more where they came from.

"Among other important underground family companies, the Bach clan ranked high in Moscow, because of both the scale of its activities and the amount of its assets. The eldest member and head of the clan was Isaak Bach."[6]

All the proletariat's representatives have to do is liquidate the exploiting class to be free of them, says Marxism. "Here was a businessman of the old generation:

104

before the Revolution, he had savored the joys of legal commerce in his father's company. During the New Economic Policy after the Revolution, when private enterprise was permitted for a short while, his commercial abilities were fully developed. The notions and ladies' underwear shops of Bach & Sons were then located on Moscow's Kuznetsky Most street, amid the city's most expensive and fashionable stores. But the New Economic Policy soon liquidated the company, confiscating its merchandise and sending its head to the camps on the Solovetsky Islands."

That's the end of Bach's incentives and capital, right? "When Bach returned from the camps in the mid-1930s, he set about creating a new family company — this time, illegal. By the late 1940s, Isaak Bach, nominally a humble workshop supervisor in a zipper and safety-pin factory at 160 rubles a month, was head of a company owning at least a dozen factories manufacturing underwear, souvenirs, and notions, and operating a network of stores in all the republics of the Soviet Union. He held assets assessed by the prosecution expert at approximately 87 million rubles."[7]

No shortage of Russian millionaires seems to be evident. In fact, like poker players, we can "see the 87 million" and "raise to 200 million," topping example with example.

"In the 1960s, two of the younger generation of that clan — Boris Roifman and his cousin Peter Order — were seized by the KGB. Both had been in underground business for about ten years. One turned over about 200 million rubles' worth of valuables to the authorities, and the other about three-quarters that amount." See and raise the 200 millions? "If three comparatively young members of the Roifman clan had amassed 350 million rubles, what might the whole family's fortune amount to, after decades in business?"[8]

Nor did these robber barons of the Russian 1960s lack any style or panache compared to their 1880s U.S. forebears. "The chief investigator of the KGB Central Office asked the wealthier of the two, 'What did you need 200 million rubles for?' Peter Order replied, with a show of bravado, 'Only 200 million! I had wanted to make 220 million — one ruble from each Soviet Citizen.'"[9]

Returning to Russian millionaires later, and how they manage to dispose of their income, the real question for an economist — counter or otherwise — is where do they find their market?

The Russian Real Market

The Counter-Economy thrives in North America mostly in "forbidden fruit" areas and those taxed to death. In Europe and Asia we can also add the overcoming of restraint of trade of otherwise legitimate foreign goods — protectionism and its complement, smuggling. But in the Second World of Communist states, two other sources arise: consumer black-ward goods' quality and reliability and their availability, something most North Americans take for granted.

"The parallel market offers not only better, usually foreign-made, clothing or rare editions of popular authors, but also provides Soviet citizens in a position to pay with better medical care, better education and training, better vacations, better interior decorating for their apartments, better babysitting facilities, better transportation, even identification papers, diplomas, and other documents. More than that, not only private individuals but governmental firms, agencies, and collective farms frequently use services of the parallel market in their efforts to obtain equipment, spare parts, manpower, and professional expertise."[10]

Consider the problem — as it is in the U.S.S.R. — of driving an automobile. Remember, while reading the following portrayal, that cars are in short supply to begin with and probably require a bribe to obtain. Now try driving it — without the Counter-Economy.

"There is a shortage of service stations in the Soviet Union and those which exist just don't have spare parts. A friend of mine spent a month in an effort to buy a windshield for his Moskvitch. All in vain."

Unlike police, there is usually a counter-economist when you need one. "Finally he came to a small street, near an automobile plant in Moscow, where he was approached by somebody who introduced himself as a worker at this plant and promised to deliver the windshield the same day for a reasonable compensation

106

— even less than the official price. Needless to say, the worker kept his promise."[11]

One also gets what one pays for in the Counter-Economy, so reliability is important in attracting consumers. (Of course, the governments in all countries spend fortunes on propaganda to convince you of the unreliability of black marketeers — and the unfailing reliability of government services.) Examples abound here. "A car owner in Armavir in southern Russia sent a letter to a driver's magazine, reporting that he was refused help at a service station. 'But then, a worker standing nearby chimed in: let him bring it in, he said. I'll fix it quickly.' And the 'sharpeared' mechanic carried out the job on the spot, pricing it at six rubles. 'Five rubles for me, and one for the till.'"[12] Six rubles would be cheap at a U.S. garage.

And again: "Another driver, from the Crimean city of Yevpatoria, complained that, although he parked his car first at the service station, attendants did not pay any attention to him and started to inspect other autos, which arrived later, presumably because their drivers had promised good tips. His protests did not help and according to the letter from this customer, the things he saw and heard there made him wonder whether it was a state enterprise or a private concern."[13]

Obviously it was the latter. Some may find it encouraging that there's a paradise where the masses know how to scorn an economic law-abider… though Russia may not have been where they thought to look for it. But an important point in the first example is missed if one ignores the necessity of conducting the business counter-economically.

"Thousands of business executives have been put in jail for alleged violations of the Soviet legislation. Many of these trials would look rather peculiar to a foreigner. The thing is that, in quite a few such cases, even the prosecution did not insist that defendants took a penny for themselves. The accused were stealing, selling at the parallel market, and buying stolen goods, not in order to make a fortune but just to get necessary supplies for their enterprises and collective farms."[14]

That last statement, to be sure, is devastating. If true, the reality of the market has smashed the facade of communism, as Marxists like to put it, objectively. And this reality penetrates to the finest details.

"Literaturnya Gazeta tells about two collective farm chairmen, convicted for buying stolen property from thieves. One purchased desperately needed pipes for a crew-shed; the other, boxes to pack apples. Significantly, no personal profit was involved in either case. Both collective farm chairmen, presumably, did not have a chance to get pipes and boxes through normal state supply channels. One of these chairmen later asked in desperation: which is more criminal — to pay thousands of rubles to thieves or to lose a harvest? This was the real alternative he faced."[15]

In a showdown between the objective forces of the market and the subjective forces of statist ideology, the former is as inexorable as the "forces of history" are supposed to be to a Marxist. "There was a meat store close to a place where I used to live in Moscow. For many years, this store was known for having an unusually good choice of meat. But, suddenly, steaks, lamb legs, and other rare items disappeared. Salesmen told the story of an old director, a Jew without a high school education but well-adjusted to unofficial rules of the Soviet trade, who was replaced by a Plekhanov's Economic Institute graduate. The new director declared that he would not tolerate any violations of law in his store. He refused to bribe district warehouse officials and, consequently, supplies of meat were almost cut off. The salesmen could no longer make a living by taking fees from grateful customers for whom they used to save good pieces of meat. Previously, they had shared their underground income with the former director, providing him with much-needed reserves of unregistered cash. Now the practice was stopped. But, without free cash, the director was unable to pay truck drivers for unloading their trucks and the drivers refused to do it free."

And so the market responded to the director's ideological pronouncements. "Both truck drivers and salesmen, angered by the new regulations, began to complain to district party committee. The former director would easily take care of such charges, merely bribing the district committee officials. But the new one found himself in real trouble. More, without supplies of good meat, his store was failing to fulfill the plan. Everyone was sure that, soon, the director would be dismissed." A happy ending to this tale? "But it did not happen. On the contrary, steaks, lambs, partridges reappeared in the store. There was no need to ask how it happened. It was clear that the young economist finally learned the real rules of Soviet trade that he had not been taught at the Plekhanov Institute."[16]

How It's Done

The simplest of economic studies informs us that one needs customers, labor, and capital goods. One can use one's own labor, take goods available — say, on the factory where one ostensibly works, and find customers in passersby, relatives, and friends. This is done in the Soviet Union, as it is everywhere else. But the more interesting cases, which document the activity of largescale counter-economic activity, need distribution networks, hired laborers, and trade with others for capital goods (production). How is that done in Russia today?

One can buy an existing business, but even that is not simple "when the owner-sellers have no rights in law."[17] One actually buys a network of connections and the trust of those countereconomists. But it can be done, with the all-important acceptance of reasonable risk, and is done.

"The prospective purchaser obviously has no way of previously assessing the enterprise's potential production, sales, or income. Buying and selling underground enterprises thus can succeed only in an atmosphere of complete trust among all parties and respect for the unwritten laws of the milieu. In this atmosphere, the purchaser hands over to the seller, with no receipt and no witnesses, tens — often hundreds — of thousands of rubles. In a case where the parties do not trust one another, the money is transferred to a third party trusted by both principals, and he passes it on to the seller only when all conditions of the sale have been met."[18]

Those even superficially acquainted with Western business may note that, save for the increased risk from a hostile State, the method is similar to that practiced in the West. In fact, all economic activities can be practiced counter-economically when the risks are acceptable.

The fascination of Counter-Economics, besides that arising from its freer nature than that of approved, regulated, and controlled business, comes from the modification to standard business practices whatever they are, as they change in time and space. As we have seen and will see, it is quite possible that the modifications to reduce risk or even outright scofflawing may be cheaper — far cheaper — than submission and compliance. The implications of that will be dealt with at the end of the book.

Delving into the inner machinery of large-scale counter-economic business is difficult. Existing ones have little incentive to "blow their cover" even in Western publications, which, after all, are readily available and scanned by the KGB, if not the DCMSP. But the Lazar Glazenberg case did reveal the workings of that medium-size operation which, although finally broken, operated successfully for a long time. The Glazenberg brothers, by the way, even had a board of directors.[19]

Here, in lengthy detail, since the core of our case is being demonstrated, is how it worked:

"The position of those officially in charge of the factories housing the Glazenbergs' enterprises was unusual: they exercised no control over the production and economic activities of their enterprises, this control being assumed by the Glazenbergs or their appointed managers. The official directors' functions were purely decorative and boiled down to liaison with party and state organs. Through trusted agents, the Glazenbergs normally paid them 500 to 1000 rubles a month, depending on the size of the enterprise and the usefulness of the director. One of their operations was run under the cover of the Fisherman-Sportsman Sporting Goods Co. in Moscow, and they paid its director 1,500 rubles a month because he held the important title of Hero of the Soviet Union."[20]

So much for the "bosses." How about the working class? "Obviously, the complicity of many blue-collar workers is also required in the manufacture of left-hand goods. It is almost impossible to recruit an entire labor force on the basis of total trust, but the Glazenberg system contrived its own incentives. The laborers knew full well that goods were being produced off the books, but they were interested in the extra money paid for left-hand production — higher than the official rates and not subject to taxation."[21]

And how about the capital goods needed? "The Glazenberg brothers cooperated with other underground businesses: clasps for handbags, buttons for leather jackets, and labels were all manufactured to their specifications by underground enterprises in Moscow, Vilnius, and Riga. But the main source of materials — and here the Glazenbergs were no different from other underground enterprises — was the factory itself: materials saved from what the factory received for its official production — that is, materials stolen from the state."[22]

The Soviet State was particularly interested in this alleged theft; after all, it uses remarkably similar means, morally speaking, in acquiring those goods in the first place (as do all states). We may thank the diligent prosecutor for the rest of our information.

"The quantity of off-the-books merchandise produced from these 'saved' materials provoked the major arguments between prosecution and defense during the trial. The point was vital to the defendants, for the quantity of materials saved for left-hand production would determine the gravity of the judgments against them — from 15 years in prison to death.

"The prosecution was able to prove that reserves were prepared in advance to yield secret surpluses. In the planning stages for production of a new product, the Glazenbergs would negotiate with the people in laboratories or institutes responsible for setting the factory's norms for new materials needed as well as for allowable wastage. In return for large bribes, these technicians deliberately inflated the usage and waste norms, thus allowing the creation of huge surpluses for manufacture of merchandise off the books.

"Other sorts of secret economies were made during the manufacturing process. Expert witnesses testified in court that they had measured coats and jackets legally manufactured at the factory, and the measurements did not tally with the sizes on the labels, because the factory's cutters had reduced the size of each pattern piece. Chemists testified that they had analyzed the artificial leather legally produced by the Glazenberg factory: the quantities of dyes and other ingredients fell short of the official specifications."[23]

Finally, let us stick with the Glazenbergs a little longer and solve the last and crucial problem: distribution.

"One would think that in a country like the Soviet Union, where trade and both the wholesale and retail levels is a state monopoly, the large-scale marketing of left-hand merchandise would simply not be feasible. The Glazenbergs proved otherwise. When the brothers were beginning in business and their only product was shopping bags, it was easy to solve the problem of how to sell the left-hand bags. Employers of shops selling the factory's output were quite willing to accept for sale a certain quantity of illegally produced bags as well. Of the proceeds, one-third went to the shop employees, two-thirds to the Glazenbergs.

"As the business grew and the range of their wares broadened, the Glazenbergs' sales outlets had to grow too. Through friends and family connections, they added to their network stores that had not been supplied with their factory's official merchandise. In time, even this network of retailers proved too small for the Glazenberg empire. So a special marketing group was established — to travel the country and in short order to organize sales outlets in 64 towns and regions."[24]

Counter Reaction to Counter-Economics

"The Soviet regime scarcely can feel comfortable with the huge scale of the parallel market activities. First of all, a totalitarian state, by its very nature, cannot appreciate any initiative coming from outside the institutional system. It sees such initiatives as a threat to its control over the economy and the people. A totalitarian state does not like it when some of its citizens become, at least partly, financially independent from the regime — when their fortunes do not totally depend on the State."[25]

Dropping the words "Soviet" and "totalitarian" in the above paragraph changes nothing. No State appreciates initiative by its citizens outside its control. See chapters one and two to begin with. What is significant here is the helplessness of the State toward counter-economic activity and the potency of the individuals. This is not just "power to the people" but power to the individual person.

And the most totalitarian expression of collectivism cannot crush it. Worse, the CounterEconomy corrodes, corrupts, splinters, and ultimately smashes the State. Besides winning away its citizens and restoring "public goods" (tax plunder) to the "private sector," "The black market also causes serious economic distortions and interferes with official economic plans. From the point of view of governmental economic agencies, equipment and supplies, which are obtained at the parallel market by some energetic managers, could be needed more and could be used more effectively by other firms and enterprises."[26] But that "need" is in the judgment of the State's planners; the people have spoken, counter-economically, that the need — demand — is otherwise and overruled the entire Soviet State.

"Moral considerations are also a factor here. Underground activities with their secret operations create far-reaching psychological consequences for large sectors of the Soviet populace. And private enterprise is absolutely inconsistent with an official communist ideology."[27] The mighty Soviet State must not only put up with the Counter-Economy but put up with its encroachment on its territory and people.

Far worse. The Soviet leadership itself is not free of counter-economic taint. "It is fair to say, while authorities are basically opposed to the parallel market, they are forced to live with it and, sometimes, do not hesitate to use it."[28] Both Pravda and Literaturnya Gazeta report authorities ordering underlings to seek out face-saving (and other-saving) parts and other capital goods in the Counter-Economy. "Literaturnya Gazeta tells about officials, pressuring collective farm chairmen to go to the parallel market. According to the paper, these officials suggest to the chairmen whose farms are short of spare parts for agricultural machinery to fish for parts 'at the bottom of the sea' but to fulfill plans. They even promise chairmen their sponsorship in case of any trouble with the police. The story carried by Literaturnya Gazeta also tells about construction managers who did not get nails but were advised by their superiors to fulfill plans at any cost."[29]

It should be stressed here that it is not only the segment of the Counter-Economy that the U.S.S.R. considers illegal, or, segments that, say, the U.S. allows that is involved, but all the Counter-Economy. A lurid example is provided by Simes that could apply to U.S.'s CIA, France's Deuxieme Bureau or SDECE, and Britain's MI6.

"Prostitution is illegal in the Soviet Union. But the KGB co-opt many prostitutes dealing with foreigners, and prostitutes paid in foreign currency surrender part of their earnings to the KGB cashier."[30] The official people's pimp?

And it should be stressed that the free market does not grow because government gets more liberal (or libertarian); rather, the counter-economic defiance of the people forces the State's retreat in order to hang on to what power it can. "Generally speaking, during recent years some kind of tolerance, if not approval, has developed in the Soviet Union regarding certain kinds of parallel market activities."[31] Next thing you know, we'll hear Izvestia will give countereconomists a sympathetic hearing and Leonid Brezhnev will call for repeal of economic laws.

"In an editorial introduction written by Izvestiya to an article about two engineers who get in trouble with authorities for precisely such actions, editorial writers have clear sympathy with the people who were forced to break the law in order to do 'their important job' properly. Both article and editorial as well as numerous other statements made by Soviet journalists and officials, including General-Secretary Brezhnev, call to eliminate 'unjustified limitations and small-minded regulation' imposed on the economic management."[32] What more can one say?

The One Failure of the Counter-Economy

There is a problem and a question yet left to be answered about the massive Soviet CounterEconomy, and the answers will bear strongly on the analysis and study of the rest of the world's Counter-Economy. Before answering, one should point out that only a narrow definition of economics has been dealt with so far and much of the Soviet Counter-Economy, the underground intellectuals, the famous "dissidents" in all the arts and humanities, have been shortchanged here.

114

Still, they have much more coverage in the Western media than strictly-business activities, which have only the pitifully few sources footnoted here.

Smuggling and refugees also have a chapter to themselves. Other references to the rich — counter-economically speaking — material and example source of Communist-controlled countries will be found sprinkled in the remaining chapters, which are categorical rather than geographical. Geographical divisions are, counter-economically at least, largely irrelevant. At least politically, counter-economists are determinedly, defiantly, even scornfully, international.

The problem cited is this: What do the wealthy counter-economists do with their wealth? There are two answers to that, and the second bears on the question yet to be asked, which is "Why doesn't the Counter-Economy become the Economy?"

First, the wealthier Eastern counter-economists may sometimes be able to leave with their money and enjoy the pleasure spots of the rest of the world. Even Russia has Riviera-like areas on the Black Sea, but ostentation in the latter requires explanation to officials. True, and more often than many would think, making the wealth, reinvesting it, and making more is a prized end in itself. James Garner's character in the 1963 film The Wheeler Dealers expressed it as "making money is just a way of keeping score" and that's in relatively free, wideopen Texas. Even so, millionaires in the West are legendary for concealing their wealth — Getty, Hughes, Koch, and other reticents are as common as the ostentations of Hearst, Hunt, and Hammer. The Western official confiscator has only a slightly shorter leash than his Eastern colleague.

Still, blowing a wad in Brezhnevland is the pits. "The Soviet underground millionaire's principal aim it not to spend money, but to conceal it."[33] Georgia, homeland of Stalin and privileged, is not too bad: II But the range is enormous: the underground millionaire's lifestyle in Moscow or Odessa, for example, is very different from his counterpart's life-style in Georgia.

"One Georgian client of mine, Golidze, who was tried by the Georgia Supreme Court, openly and legally owned two magnificent houses. Both were luxuriously furnished with antiques bought from dealers in Moscow and Leningrad. During a search, authorities confiscated his wife's jewelry, and 45,000 rubles in cash — which Golidze explained to me was just lying around at home to cover day-to-day expenses."[34]

So things are tighter in other Red lands? "The Georgian life-style is not remotely appreciated by underground millionaires in Moscow, the Ukraine, and the Baltic Republics. Forsaking the communal apartment bought under his own name, where he can enjoy expensive foods without having to hide them from the neighbors ... buying a modest dacha under a relative's name ... or taking a trip to a Bulgarian resort on the Black Sea ... all this is about the extent of pleasures that a millionaire of the older generation dare allow himself. His principal entertainment is getting together with male colleagues in private, and the eternal male need for a bit of fun outside the family circle is satisfied by several salons maintained by women with social or business connections with the underground milieu. The attraction of these salons is gambling rather than sex."[35]

One can readily see that providing entertainment for the fun-loving, wealthier countereconomists is itself logically, a counter-economic enterprise. "During the 1960s and 1970s, the salon of one Elizabeth Mirkien enjoyed great popularity in Moscow. Her husband had been in the employ of one of the large underground companies and was at the time serving a prison sentence. In the spirit of the unwritten laws of the milieu, the husband's partners were providing Elizabeth with a decent sum of money each month, but she also had an income from the salon of her small two-room apartment. Middle-aged businessmen liked to assemble there. Everything was to their liking: the head of the house herself, a handsome and affable lady; excellent meals; and, above all, the card tables and roulette wheel. The stakes were very high, for games of chance occupy a very important place in the life of a wealthy underground Soviet businessman. Only at the card table or the roulette wheel in some house such as Elizabeth's are they able to risk huge losses, feel the euphoria of spending recklessly, feel rich."[36] And yet, save quantitatively, is that a different attitude from that found in Monte Carlo or Las Vegas?

Why does the Counter-Economy not become the economy? The one failure of the CounterEconomy so far, is on the mental-spiritual-psychological level — the abstract level. As we shall see, the scientists and engineers of abstraction, the intellectuals, have failed so far to analyze and justify the Counter-Economy. Thus Counter-Economists operate under the dead weight of unearned guilt. The effort to change this around, to provide the Counter-Economy with a fullblown, self-justifying philosophy — agorism — has just begun.[37]

Nonetheless, the guilt and self-inhibition is evident in Russia as in the West. "The oldergeneration millionaires, beyond indulging in such pleasures, try to shield their children from the risks of the underground world and make them into academics, doctors or lawyers."[38] That is to say, the children are to be made respectable and above-ground. This thinking and the failure to generate, so far, a supply of pro-market ideology, is the failure of the Counter-Economy.

The Hope of the Future

But the children, the second generation counter-economists, are showing signs of appreciating the innovation and courage of their forebears — more than the forebears did — and may themselves conclude the liberation. Their parents try to get them out and into Communist acceptability. "Despite this, many children — after university degrees, even doctorates — reaffirm the family tradition and enter underground business. These second- and third-generation underground businessmen are not content with the lives of their fathers. They become habitués of expensive restaurants, whose waiters and managers know them by name, treat them as honored guests — and report their binges to the DCMSP. They are not afraid to make large bets at the races, watched by DCMSP agents, or too timid to buy cars and dachas at prices equivalent to 20 to 30 years of their official salaries. They openly visit fashionable resorts, spending five years' official salary on a month's vacation."[39]

Nor is their defiance and "coming out" folly or self-destructive bravado. From their parents' knees, these New Counter-Economists know what they are doing, and their ingenuity surpasses their teachers.

"This does not mean that the younger generation of underground businessmen are lunatics prepared to trade one year of high living for many years in the prison camps. They all try to be prepared to justify their expenditures by pointing to some sort of legal income. A common way is to buy a lottery ticket or

117

government loan bond that has had a big win. The biggest of the younger businessmen retain paid agents among bank employees who persuade winners who come to pick up their money to sell the lucky ticket for two to three times the amount of the win. But the main insurance for the younger generation remains the bribing of DCMSP officials — at which they outdo even their parents."[40]

When everyone is linked by self-interest to their fellow counter-economists, in whole or part, in Russia or anywhere, and they are fully aware of this, the Counter-Economy will inescapably succeed. The base is there. "According to the Soviet Writers Union weekly, Literaturnya Gazeta, during only year, occupants of new Moscow apartments paid ten million rubles to private tradesmen for 'additional improvements to their apartment.'"[41]

Them And Us

Confirmation of this state of affairs in the Union of Soviet Socialist Republics comes from the most Establishment of sources — The New York Times Russian correspondent, Hedrick Smith, observed: "Corruption and illegal private enterprise in Russia, 'creeping capitalism,' as some Russians playfully call it, grow out of the very nature of the Soviet economy and its efficiencies — shortages, poor quality goods, terrible delays in service. They constitute more than a black market, as Westerners are accustomed to thinking of it. For parallel to the official economy, there exists an entire, thriving counter-economy which handles an enormous volume of hidden or semi-hidden trade that is indispensable for institutions as well as individuals. Practically any material or service can be arranged nalevo [nalevo means 'on the left,' but comes across as 'on the side' or 'under the table'] — from renting a holiday cottage in the country, buying a raincoat or a good pair of shoes in a state store, getting a smart dress made by a good seamstress,
transporting a sofa across town, having the plumbing fixed or sound-proofing installed on your apartment door, being treated by a good dentist, sending your children to a private playschool, arranging home consultation with a top-flight surgeon, to erecting buildings and laying pipe in a collective farm."[42]

As we have seen in the first two chapters, Westerners are rapidly becoming accustomed to thinking of a far wider counter-economy. All the sources mentioned in this chapter convey this feeling of difference — which is valid — but with an implication of qualitative rather than quantitative difference. "Setting aside such sensational cases of abusing official positions, only a small part of the operations of the Soviet counter-economy would be considered criminal in the West. To be sure, the Soviet Union has embezzlers, car theft rings, prostitutes, narcotics traffickers, armed bank robbers, and an occasional band of extortionists posing as police units complete with uniforms, handcuffs and documents, shaking down the innocent — offenders who would be criminals anywhere." Including, it must be added, in the Counter-Economy itself. Smith's list is the red market of violence and coercion, not the peaceful, state-dodging black market. He continues, "But much of the private hustling on the black market would not be illegal if Soviet Communism permitted the kind of small private trade sector that exists legally under Hungarian, Polish, or East German brands of Communism."[43]

Such naivete is interesting for the many things it tells us. While it's true that releasing some of human action as is done in the other East European countries would reduce the counter-economy slightly, Smith seems unaware how vast it is there. Furthermore, he is unaware, it seems, how vast it is in New York City, his home base. Because New York is more highly regulated than the rest of the U.S. in many respects — taxi medallions, higher tax rates, for example — it swarms with gypsy cabs, unlicensed food vendors, non-union carpenters and movers, tobacco bootleggers, or "buttleggers," and dealers in all illicit substances and prohibited copies (computer programs to records). Perhaps, like the New Class of Communist aristocrats he portrays in their closed-off suburbs away from the suffering Moscow masses, he belongs to a class which avoids such street contact.[44]

Smith does perceive, at least dimly, the revolutionary possibilities. "But the regime faces a dilemma: As one Russian, echoed by many others, observed to me, 'Everyone in the Soviet retail trade is a thief and you can't put them all in jail.'" And yet he confuses reform with revolution near the end. "The Party knows, he reasoned, that people who are chasing after illegal goods in the counter-economy are not worried about reforms. Moreover so long as the public takes the counter-economy as a necessary and desirable fact of life, there is scant hope of collaboration for strict enforcement."[45]

The resolution in the Russian — and Western — mind of this dichotomy could well end the statism in favor of a complete Counter-Economy. Of course, it would then be the economy, a free market. Smith has an anecdote which illustrates the confusion of economic efficiency and freedom with anti-social inhumanity.

"A medical scientist who emigrated to America in 1974 after working at one of Moscow's leading medical institutes praised Russian doctors as 'more humane' than profit-oriented private physicians in America and endorsed the concept of socialized medicine. 'But you cannot imagine how poor is the general quality of medical service,' he said. 'In Rejazan (a city of 400,000) where I grew up, they have very bad equipment. They lacked very simple things — medicines for example. The qualification of the doctors is much lower than in Moscow. But the worst problem in the system is poor organization and bad nursing service. The nurses do sterilization very badly. After operations, even in our institute which is one of the very top ones, we had a lot of sepsis, festering wounds, infections, and suppuration. The nurses were not clean enough. They made mistakes in operations. Our institute director became very angry because he would do beautiful operations, and then there were those infections. So often, you know, the middle-level personnel do not receive good pay and they are not reliable, not competent. Once I was in Kharkov and I had to be operated on for appendicitis in an ordinary district hospital. It was so dirty that you cannot imagine it. The sheets were grey from such long use. The clothes of the hospital workers were not clean enough. They took special care of me because I was from this important institute in Moscow. Still I got an infection and so did others. I saw one man die in my presence after an appendicitis operation because of this problem."[46]

This is the overground economy in the most statist area in the world. Small wonder people seek cold, profit-seeking marketeers who turn out clean, precise, antiseptic operations in mass production cheaply — or if they are prevented, they will seek out black marketeers who will do it less cheaply but give the customer what he or she wants. Says Dimitri Simes, "The parallel market is a vital part of the Soviet way of life. And only fundamental economic and social reforms can wipe it out of existence."[47] But can they be fundamental enough, that is, will the State abolish itself?

The forces of the market, overwhelming the Marxist-religious Forces of History, may leave no choice. Although Konstantin Simis implies corruption — counter-economizing the statists themselves — is avoidable, his conclusion speaks for itself in reply: "And there appears one final revealing absurdity. Obviously, the Soviet state and the whole structure of underground enterprise are pitted against each other in absolute conflict and contradiction. Yet these adversaries are weirdly allied. They are bound by corruption. There could be no vast labyrinth of lawless enterprise — not for a year, not even a month — without the complicity and the venality of the equally vast Soviet apparatus charged with enforcing the laws against economic crime. This official criminality is all-pervasive, from the lowest officialdom to the highest elite — a cancer plaguing not just the state but all of Soviet society. This is the awesome cost of a system dedicated to stifling the most basic impulses of personal freedom."[48]

That system is not Sovietism, or even Communism, but statism. It exists and is growing in North America. In the next few chapters, we shall see how North Americans — and, now and then, the rest of the world, deals with a world of bureaucracy and nalevo — of legal plunder and illegal production. First we'll look at the biggest network of small entrepreneurs in the CounterEconomy, the drug market in all its aspects and definitions of what drugs are, and then the biggest problem of Counter-Economics in East and West alike: money and its control and the ravages of inflation.

Footnotes

1. Free market cracks Red regimes. (1976, July 25). New Libertarian Weekly 3(33) p. 1.
2. Simes, D. K. (1975). The Soviet parallel market. Washington, DC: Center for Strategic and International Studies, Georgetown University, p. 25.
3. Simis, K. (1981, June 29). Russia's underground millionaires. Fortune, p. 37.
4. Ibid., pp. 38-39.
5. Ibid.
6. Ibid.

7. Ibid.

8. Ibid.

9. Ibid.

10. Simes, D. K. op. cit., p. 70.

11. Ibid.

12. Ibid., p. 7.

13. Ibid.

14. Ibid., p. 16.

15. Ibid., p. 17.

16. Ibid., p. 18.

17. Simis, K. op. cit., p. 40.

18. Ibid., p. 41.

19. Ibid.

20. Ibid.

21. Ibid.

22. Ibid.

23. Ibid., pp. 41-42.

24. Ibid., p. 42.

25. Simes, D. K. op. cit., p. 21.

26. Ibid.

27. Ibid.

28. Ibid., p. 22.

29. Ibid., pp. 23-24.

30. Ibid., p. 24.

31. Ibid.

32. Simis, K. op. cit., p. 49.

33. Ibid.

34. Ibid.

35. Ibid.

36. See, for example, J. Neil Schulman's novel, Alongside Night (Crown hardcover, 1979; Ace paperback August 1982).

37. Simis, K. op. cit., p. 47.

38. Ibid.

39. Ibid.

40. Simes, D. K., op. cit., p. 1, footnote 1.

41. Smith, H. (1977). The Russians. New York: Ballantine Books, pp. 112-113. Chapter Three is entirely devoted to Counter-Economics in Russia, and Smith is the first person after myself I have found to use the term "counter-economy," although he does not use "Counter-Economics" or "counter-economist." A communication with him revealed no knowledge of my prior use from February, 1974 (before an audience of the Free Market Forum in California, and subsequently in hundreds of libertarian publications). His book, by the by, is recommended.

42. Ibid., p. 132.

43. While Smith lived in Russia, the author lived in New York's East Village in a cluster of apartments of hard-core counter-economists and worked counter-economically with New Zealand and Australian illegal aliens, during the period 1972-1975.

44. Smith, op. cit., p. 133.

45. Ibid., pp. 94-95.

46. Simes, D. K., op. cit., p. 25.

47. Simis, K. op. cit., p. 50.

4. Drug Counter-Economics

To many people, illicit drugs and black market are strongly connected. The case for the existence of the counter-economy of drug consumption, production, agriculture, distribution network, financing, transportation, and smuggling, and even its use as an alternate currency has been made in the popular press from High Times to *the New York Times.*

Rather than making the counter-economic understanding of the drug market easier to convey for the author, the preconceptions and prejudices involved make it the most difficult chapter in the book. Nonetheless, the issue is best tackled forthrightly and immediately. The problem is not the mechanics — though that is often misrepresented, as we shall see — but the intense irrationality surrounding the subject. Drug abuse is a term in great need of *disabuse.*

Drug Disabuse

If we discussed the marketing of acetylsalicylic acid to beat Bayer Aspirin's monopoly prices, few would be disturbed. Can we abuse "aspirin?" Medical experts suggest that an excess causes stomach bleeding, so it seems possible. Acetylsalicylic acid is a pharmaceutical item, sold in "drug stores." Where is the "aspirin abuse problem?"

Let us look at tobacco. While heavily restricted in marketing by anti-advertising regulation and taxed higher than anything else, it remains "legal." Nicotine, tobacco's most active ingredient, is rated somewhere between caffeine and tetrahydrocannabinol (coffee and pot) in social acceptance, and is as much a "drug" as either. Today it is still legal and a much-maligned nonproblem.

Should the final step toward outlawing of cigarettes and pipes be taken tomorrow, it would undoubtedly touch off a civil war in North America. While smokers have been "taking it," in the form of constant nagging in the media and petty harassment at cocktail parties as long as they could get their "fix," they would flagrantly and massively disobey any laws stopping them from obtaining it. Remember, a majority of people — not just adults — of both sexes and all races outside the most poverty-stricken parts of the world smoke tobacco.

One step from aspirin to tobacco, another to alcohol. Booze was slightly less popular and slightly more "powerful" (disabling when over-consumed) and actually did meet with an era of Prohibition.

Prohibition was not defeated by political reform, organized revolution, or even street activists — though all were around in the United States in the 1920s. What is almost universally known is that it was abundantly and easily available at a price little different from the legal, taxed price, and the "cost" of entering this market — in terms of additional risk — was so low that one often drank in front of senators and even sheriffs with impunity.

The failure of Prohibition to prohibit was the most spectacular triumph of Counter-Economics in the United States. Alcohol "in moderation" (whatever that is) is now almost completely acceptable.

Alas, it is almost totally "white market" and taxed to death, second only to the taxation of tobacco products.

Let us take one more step to marijuana along the drug spectrum. Tetrahydrocannabinol, at least as found in joints (as opposed to hash oil) is less powerful than alcohol. Yet its popular acceptance is lower; that is, its use is not enjoyed by a majority in the democratic countries. Hence, it is illegal.

The Counter-Economy sector connected with marijuana is so large that it touches nearly every man, woman, and child in North America (and much of the rest of the world). This claim will be backed up in the next section; a different point is being made here.

Let us skip over one drug spectrum step: what about arsenic and cyanide? These substances are not only not illegal but not even all that controlled. Is there any proscribed drug as capable of harm with as few "redeeming" side effects ? Why are not cyanide and arsenic the most persecuted drugs of all? People do take them. But in almost all journalese you will never hear about "another arsenic-related death" Or "cyanide abuse." The usual term is suicide.

125

Whatever the potency and "threat" of heroin, opium, lysergic acid diethylamide, or amphetamines — and they lie between alcohol and arsenic by anyone's estimate — they are something "special" in the eyes of a large sector of society with considerable political clout. Is it a Puritan hatred of pleasure, then? How about the prohibition of Laetrile (which is also faltering at the time of this writing)?

Drugs are not a poison unless chosen for that use. They are not a cure unless chosen for that use. They are not agents of pleasure or escape or stimulation unless chosen for that use. In short, the chemicals are irrelevant to any "drug problem" — drug abuse is *choice abuse*.

What one should choose is a religious problem, in the broadest sense of the term. Choosing the wrong drugs (and almost everyone chooses some, however "mild" or innocuous) is exactly like choosing the wrong religion a couple of centuries ago — you are an infidel, heretic, or heathen and you will be hunted down and persecuted. You will also be aided, befriended, and even hidden from your persecutors by sympathizers with your beliefs.

There is one major difference between most commonly understood religious practices and the use of drugs: the trade in physical goods. While there is a giant market in religion, outlawing associated material goods merely pinches the believers a bit and often hardens their convictions.

Outlawing drugs discourages a few marginal buyers but just as often hardens the users and deepens their commitment. Would there exist the marijuana-based counter-culture or laetrilebased, mostly right-wing, movement if the State had not suppressed their drugs-of-choice?

And, of course, the line between drug culture and religion has actually been crossed many times: peyote-based Indian and neo-Indian hippie sects, the marijuana (ganja)-based Rastafarians, and the numerous "accepted" religions that use wine (persecuted during Prohibition) or food rules and dietary restrictions (Orthodox Jews and fundamentalist Christians).

One's choice of religion has become, largely, and in most countries, no longer the business of the State. At least in the more enlightened countries of the West, one's choice of drugs is being perceived more and more as a question of individual conscience. Until this view prevails, the drug market is the greatest single recruiting and consciousness-raising sector of the CounterEconomy, with the exception of tax avoidance.[1]

The Drug Capital Pyramid

To understand the vastness of the interconnectedness of the drug market, one needs to introduce an important concept of economics, and to discard a misconception mostly spawned by the propaganda of the Drug Wars fought by several levels and agencies of the State. The latter is the myth of the mob or "organized crime;" the former is the concept of the capital pyramid. One is, in a sense, the mirror-image or perversion of the other.

The term "organized crime" says too much. If you and your neighbors work together to beat taxes or the draft or distribute and consume drugs — anything the State considers a crime — you are a "conspiracy;" that is, by not working solo, you have committed an additional crime. You are organized criminals and the organized government (some would say disorganized government) dislikes that even more. The degree of formality of this organization can be very slight indeed. You may not even know personally those with whom you deal; you may simply meet, transact, and possibly never meet again.

The marketplace spontaneously organizes supply and demand, regardless of commodity. People need not add any ties or fondness or supportiveness to these ephemeral links but, being people, they do, and we shall delve into this awareness expansion or consciousness raising later in this chapter. The construction of a giant superstructure across many borders and in minute detail on every street of agriculture, processing, shipping, refining, wholesaling, and distribution requires no long-term conspiring or formal organization such as a syndicate or "Mafia."

Gangsters, the Mob, whatever they're called, are not the drug market or even part of the Counter Economy; rather, they are the State within the State. They prey

127

upon the countereconomists by collecting "protection" taxes, regulating trade, and fighting wars. The Cosa Nostra and the Purple Gang and such serve no function in the Counter-Economy save that of parasite in exactly the same way the official government does in the market. In certain backward communities and neighborhoods, usually some elder ethnic culture, such groups are tolerated or even supported by frightened people as real protectors, just as such authoritarian governments are accepted by the people of unenlightened countries. Yet in the "hot" drug markets of the American university campuses and Southern California in particular, such mobsters simply do not exist.

If the Godfather doesn't direct the black market, who or what does? Rather than some Sicilian's Black Hand, the market is directed — without government interference or in spite of it — by Adam Smith's Invisible Hand.

Someone realizes that people are willing to pay for drugs and that someone realizes that the price will get him or her a profit sufficient to make it worth his or her effort. Another realizes that there are these dealers who will pay well for a large amount of a drug — and will break it up for retail, marking it up to make it worth their effort. Yet someone else sees the opportunity in setting up a chemical laboratory to refine drugs and deliver them to a few wholesalers and another sees the profit in smuggling in drugs to a few refiners. And still another sees the value in supplying smugglers in their homeland from farmers in their area looking for a few extra dollars, pesos, or bat. And farmers see the value in dodging or paying off the government officials to grow a little extra of a forbidden crop.

This "vertical" market structure — from layers of producers to a base of consumers — was discovered, as an economic concept, by Eugen von Böhm-Bawerk, the greatest Austrian economist next to Ludwig Von Mises, and called the Capital Pyramid. One of Böhm-Bawerk's theories states that the more "progressive" the market, the higher the pyramid grows; that is, the base narrows and the height grows more layers. More and more wealth is transferred to earlier stages of production — yet the end product has finer quality and/or, lower price. The Capital Pyramid of the drug market rivals that of space-shuttle production — and it is growing, against a literal army of government agents, armed to the teeth and shooting.[2]

If anything can prove the unstoppable nature of the Counter-Economy, the triumph of the drug market's Capital Pyramid against the armed might of the State should. So here is some proof.

The Second World War — Against Drugs

It's been said that if Man will not learn from history, he is condemned to relive it. Two World Wars may still not have cured us of world war, but at least there's been a longer gap between them. In the 1920s, the United States imposed a Prohibition on the drug ethyl alcohol in all its forms even as various provinces in Canada were repealing local prohibition as failures. In 1933, the First World War — and it was fought across borders and on the high seas — against Demon Booze ended in surrender with the Repeal of Prohibition. Soon after, the State in all countries stepped up its suppression of thousands of other chemicals ingested by humans for pleasure, escape, or stimulation and held it seemingly at stalemate. Then came the 1960s and the new philosophies, and the rise of psychedelic drugs. A new war was declared by the State against lysergic acid diethylamide and peyote and STP, and the old one with cannabis sativa and amphetamines and tranquilizers ("uppers and downers") was redoubled.

"War" is not a metaphor here. "The U.S. Coast Guard reports that on two separate occasions in recent months, U.S. gunboats were forced to fire shots directly into the hulls of ships carrying marijuana. Coast Guard officials say this is the first time since Prohibition — almost 50 years ago — that smuggling boats have actually been fired upon and hit by Coast Guard ships in the process of making arrests.

"Commandant John Hayes says that until the two recent incidents, seizures at sea have required, at the most, a warning shot or two across the bow to force the vessel to surrender. Neither of the shooting incidents resulted in injuries. Hayes says that more and more ships are trying to outrun Coast Guard cutters because marijuana has become a big business, with single cargoes worth millions of dollars. The Coast Guard estimates that $6 to $8 billion in illicit weed was successfully smuggled by ships into the U.S. last year."[3]

The United States, largely through the Drug Enforcement Administration, has opened up fronts on the war throughout Central and South America, both ends of Asia, and Western Europe, a true World War. Yet, "home-grown" remains the biggest source of raw drug material, as our look at California and Hawaii will reveal. There's nothing foreign or alien about drug-dealing, but the market is completely international.

Colombia is described by United Press International as a "Pot Empire." Riohacha "is the capital of La Guajira state and the hub of Colombia's biggest illegal industry — growing and smuggling marijuana in the United States. It is also a key outpost in the government's battle to reduce the drug traffic, which threatens to overshadow all of the country's legitimate business."[4]

How big can this one sector of its Counter-Economy be? "Estimates of the total Colombian drug business vary, but it is generally put at around $2 billion annually. A good part of the 'pot' lands in the hands of international dealers based in the United States."[5]

Colombia is also a distribution and processing center for different drugs from different countries; it also maintains one of the largest single labor forces of the Counter-Economy "Colombia also is one of the countries where cocaine from Peru and Bolivia is processed for shipment to the United States, mainly by gangs operating out of the cities of Medellin and Cali. However, the white powder accounts for less than half the dollar value of the marijuana trade and involves a much smaller labor force than the 150,000 persons involved in 'pot' trafficking."[6]

To really get a feel for the large scale of this particular industry, one needs to absorb an eyewitness description. "At an army base outside Riohacha, soldiers in T-shirts and fatigue trousers stack scores of large bales wrapped in burlap bags. Tons of 'Santa Maria Gold,' prime marijuana from the slopes of the Santa Maria Mountains, are being prepared for a bonfire of destruction after being seized in the latest army operation.

"A dozen trucks confiscated in the action are parked in a row. A few yards away are the mangled remains of a small plane that crashed on the highway near the army base presumably when on a marijuana mission.... Through the end of June, the armed forces had seized 80 airplanes in northern Colombia, nearly all of them registered in the United States. They include a DC-7, a DC-6, a Convair, and three venerable DC-3's, along with many small twin-engine planes. Of that total, 23 planes had crashed while attempting dangerous landings on makeshift runways. A total of 72 boats, 308 vehicles, and 879 firearms were also confiscated.

"In the same period, 1,169 suspects were arrested. Of the 186 foreigners among the arrested, most were Americans. The army says it destroyed nearly 38,000 tons of marijuana, including 50,000 bales ready for shipment and the estimated yield of 25,250 acres. It also grabbed 2.2 million amphetamine tablets ready for export and 74 pounds of cocaine apparently by marijuana smugglers outside the main cocaine route."[7]

That massive drug bust must certainly have set back the Colombian drug business, right? "'We figure we have got our hands on less than 10% of the total production,' an army officer said grimly."[8] Note that 10% is lower than taxation rates in most countries.

See, in our present example, how a counter-economic Capital Pyramid builds a large community of common interest in defence of a black market. "The root of the problem is money — the dollars and pesos that convince the farmers to run the risk of raising the illegal crop and that tempt ill-paid police, soldiers, and even judges to collaborate with the drug traffic. La Guajira has long been known in Colombia as an economically depressed area where dealing in contraband is considered a normal way of life. The local populace welcomes outsiders with the same open-hearted warmth that Tennessee mountaineers reserve for internal revenue officers."[9] The comparison, as we have noted, is highly apt.

"Ernesto Samper, president of a national federation of Colombian financial institutions ... estimated that 150,000 Colombians depend on marijuana for a living and said nearly all are small farmers and their families [are] low-level drug runners. If Colombia had legalized production, he said, it could have collected nearly $146 millions in taxes last year instead of spending a comparable amount on enforcement."[10] Another solution to the taxes spent on enforcement can be found in the previous chapters.

131

This zealous state crackdown on the drug trade is atypical. Moving from the Latin American theater of this World War to the Middle Eastern theater — where Israeli, Arab, Christian, and UN soldiers abound — we see another attitude.

"Not far from where the harvesters were at work, soldiers were lazily waving cars on down the highway. To them, hashish was just another crop. Some say this is among the best hashish in the world. They call it 'Lebanese Red,' 'Lebanese Blond' and other names. It is made from the marijuana plant — Indian hemp, it is called in this part of the world — and it is marketed as oil or in flat pieces that look like the soles of heavy shoes."[11]

Except for the military attitude, the Colombian scene is repeated. "It goes out by truck and boat and plane, and is widely thought to account for as much as a third of all the money that comes into Lebanon. Lebanon has only a semblance of government, but its banks are thriving and hashish is one of the major reasons.

"'I think we can say that without a doubt "hash" is the biggest industry in the country,' a Western diplomat who tries to monitor the drug traffic here said. Exact figures are hard to come by, but it is estimated that 80% of the Bekaa Valley is given over to growing hashish. So much land is in Indian hemp that the valley, one of the richest farm areas in the world, can no longer produce all the fruits and vegetables Lebanon needs."[12]

Most legal industries are nowhere near this size. Can this one drug industry be so vast and yet prohibited by the State? "And although growing hashish is technically illegal, the harvest comes in every year right under the nose of the law — or what is left of the law. The soldier directing traffic on the road, who cannot fail to notice that the hashish is being harvested, said: 'Growing it is illegal, but it is not our job to stop it.'"13 The bureaucratic response is given to the unstoppable free market.

And the market replies. The reporter of the above scene interviewed a nearby farmer.

"He was standing at the edge of his crop, which in a few days would be harvested and then dried in a small shed. Then it would be picked up by the man who had come out earlier to inspect it, to assess the quality of the plants before agreeing on a price. 'This is the best way to feed my family,' the farmer said. 'Without hashish, I would be a poor man.'"[14]

While some may describe Lebanon's government as having broken down, there are certainly plenty of armies — most made up of religious types with strong anti-drug tenets — marching up and down the country. Even with far more governments than most people face, the CounterEconomy survives. "The story is told of a grower who keeps two military vehicles — tanks — to protect his fields. It may be an exaggeration, yet it is true that the fields are virtually never disturbed. Too many people have an interest in the crop. And it is generally accepted that the growers pay protection money to the many armed militia groups that operate in the area."[15]

The interlocking network spreads out at all vertical levels of the Capital Pyramid horizontally as well. "One expert said that some hashish is flown to neighboring Middle East states, and that some is trucked through Syria to Turkey, then on to Europe. The chief client there is said to be the Netherlands. Most of the hashish, however, is consumed in the Middle East. Egypt is the biggest buyer."[16]

The drug counter-economy includes high finance, right up to the international banking system. "The farmers and middlemen are often paid in U.S. currency that has been 'laundered' a number of times before it reaches Lebanon in an effort to throw drug agents off the scent. One source cited the example of a buyer who took an Amsterdam bank draft and deposited it in a Swiss bank. The money was transferred to Venezuela, to Taiwan, and then to a bank in one of the Persian Gulf states before it finally arrived in Beirut.

"Lebanese authorities estimate that $250 million came into the country last year in connection with the hashish trade. This year, the estimate is for twice that figure.... 'The banks are filled with money,' a Western diplomat said..."[17]

Over in the Far Eastern theater of our World War, we find a few differences on specifics but the counter-economic basics remain comfortably familiar. "Stashed

133

in airliner restrooms, sewn inside baseballs, or taped to the bodies of smugglers, Pakistani heroin is reaching U.S. and West European cities in ever-increasing quantities and causing international concern, U.S. and Pakistani officials say. Opium cultivation has dropped sharply in this valley and other major poppy-growing areas of Pakistan. But what remains is apparently more than ample for a string of underground laboratories that began producing the country's first heroin in the past year."[18]

Remembering that the Counter-Economy recognizes no state borders, we're not surprised to find full market cooperation among those of different nationalities and religious denominations up and down this Capital Pyramid. "At least five Iranian chemists were known to be in the semiautonomous tribal territory of North West Frontier where the infant heroin industry is located and where law enforcement officers have no jurisdiction."[19]

"Heroin is much easier to transport — and conceal — than raw opium extracted from poppies, and it pays to make the conversion. Ten kilograms (22 pounds) of raw opium in the currently depressed market here costs about $300 and yields a kilogram of heroin. This amount of heroin sells for about $10,000 in Pakistan, at least $45,000 in Western Europe, and $175,000 on the U.S. East Coast, a U.S. Embassy official said. Once in the hands of U.S. dealers, the heroin is cut and sold in packets. The income to such dealers runs into the millions of dollars from a single kilo."[20]

The Counter-Economy is invulnerable to the State, not by using the State's concepts of attack and defence, but by market methods — a way of thinking alien to Statists. It takes governmental actions into account, along with supply and demand.

"There is a glut of opium in Pakistan because of low prices arising from disturbed conditions in the traditional 'golden crescent' markets in Iran and Afghanistan. Guerrilla warfare has made shipping raw opium through Afghan mountain passes too risky and the death penalty imposed by the Iranian revolutionary regime on drug dealers has dampened their enthusiasm for the trade: Filling the gap, Pakistani narcotic entrepreneurs secured the refining knowhow and either used Persian Gulf sea routes or the numerous direct air links with the West to smuggle out the heroin, the sources said."[21]

The interchangeability of methods in the Counter-Economy is highly useful to entrepreneurs. Those who find the drugs involved unsavory might still learn valuable techniques for risk reduction. Within the drug industry, one product line may be instructive to another.

"'A number of Iranians operating independently have been picked up in the past year through sheer inexperience,' in the United States, said an American official. 'But the Pakistanis have been smarter by using networks which they had established earlier for hashish.' Pakistan lacks the domestic consumption on the scale of Iran in the past. But as heroin refining expands here, drug-enforcement officials fear that demand for opium will pick up."[22]

In 1980, economically depressed Jamaica threw out the socialist government and installed Edward Seaga. Part of Jamaica's problem was its chronically negative balance of payments — a balance which, naturally, did not include counter-economic exports. Seaga threatened to legalize the ganja trade and count marijuana in the balance of payments, which, nearly everyone agreed, would have given Jamaica a positive balance and gotten the International Monetary Fund bankers off its back.

Rather than accept a return to sound accounting practices and an extension of the free market — the U.S. could have always claimed a concession to the local large Jamaican religion, the Rastafarians — the U.S. hiked foreign aid and extended loans. The Rastafarians, by the way, constitute a third force in Jamaican politics, but are largely anti-political, undoubtedly from their continuous contact with the reality of the marketplace. (Rastafarians have a distribution network throughout the U.S. and U.K. thanks to the present popularity of reggae, their sect's music, which is allied to punk rock.)

The American government does not hesitate to overthrow or destabilize other States that are on the wrong side of the Second World Drug War. Bolivia's anti-communist junta, which overthrew a democratic government in 1980, was destabilized by the DEA and CIA. General Torres' problem was not his cavalier disregard for democracy and "human rights" (no government respects human rights) and certainly not his opposition to Bolivian socialism; alas, he was suspected of being the main military "protection" of the Bolivian drug industry.

A counter-economic head of state being a contradiction, General Torres did not need much additional instability. Still, the extent to which this story was accepted at face value by many respected magazines and newspapers indicates the credibility; those reporting from Bolivia and encountering its Counter-Economy are convinced it could have happened.

While the Drug Warriors lose Colombia, Lebanon, and Pakistan, and break even or hold the line in Bolivia and Jamaica, where the war will be decided is on the Home Front. Unlike the World Wars, where U.S. soil was untouched, the American statists are powerless to prevent a massive invasion of the continental United States, not to mention a massive defection to the "enemy" of much of its citizenry.

Drug Wars: The Home Front

"Federal officials say that the state of Florida would suffer a serious economic blow if the United States could halt the expanding cocaine market in the U.S. The U.S. Drug Enforcement Administration estimates that three-fourths of all the coke entering the U.S. today comes through the state of Florida; and that the street value of Florida's cocaine alone exceeds $10 billion a year.

"The Journal of the Addiction Research Foundation says that so much coke-related cash is generated in Florida that numerous Florida banks have become dependent on the illicit coke market. According to one federal official quoted by The Journal, the real estate market in Florida would "fall flat" if cocaine traffic were suddenly halted, allegedly because a high percentage of Florida's purchases of land and houses involve money stemming from the cocaine trade."[23]

The same Capital Pyramid, the same horizontal networking, and the same operational modes and risk-reduction methods as we saw around the world are evident at home in the United States, that government in the world most committed to crushing Devil Weed and Killer Coke. Still, Florida is a

136

marketplace; surely keeping out those nasty foreigners with their filthy habits (see Chapter Ten on immigration) would end the Drug Menace? Even Hawaii, the state of lavish marijuana plantations and a futures commodity market in pot crops,[24] would be cut off with a tight naval blockade?

Unfortunately for those willing to fight on the beaches, to fight on the shores, and to fight on the landing grounds, the homeland has fallen. The largest U.S. market — California — is also largely self-contained, literally from the ground up.

"In the remote hills and trackless valleys of northern California, it's time to bring in what they call here the 'happy harvest.' The grass is as high as an elephant's eye in the shimmering noonday heat. But the casual visitor rarely spots the tall, saw-toothed plants tucked away in camouflaged, booby-trapped, and guarded plots. This fall it's a bumper crop, worth somewhere between $500 million (U.S.) and $1 billion — probably the most valuable cash crop in the golden state, food bowl of America. And a lot of people — small-time pirates, the Mafia, police in helicopters, posses of sheriffs' deputies, federal narcotics agents — want to snatch it away from the growers."[25]

California drug agriculture is moving up to the level of King Cotton or "flowing oceans of golden grain;" we're talking *counties*, boy.

"The crop is common hemp, cannabis sativa — marijuana — and in the past three years it has transformed the social and economic life of a vast five-county area of northern California, which stretches from San Francisco to the Oregon border. It is, of course, illegal, but in this 16,000 square miles of rugged country, smallholders find the risks well worth the annual tax-free income of $200,000 and up that a diligent farmer can earn."[26]

Politicians are not necessarily "bought off." There are places "the potvilles of northern California, oddly named backwoods towns — Willits, Garberville, Ukiah — where conservative old-timers and sharp, young university-educated entrepreneurs have an uneasy alliance. They want the law and the political bosses in Sacramento, the state capital, to stay out of their business: in this area, long-depressed by a timber industry slump, pot is a godsend." Still, the politicians try to jump on the bandwagon. "State Senator Barry Keene announced that he was pushing a bill to decriminalize cultivation. The physical ill effects of pot were not proven, he said, 'and right now what I see is a multimillion-dollar business in the heart of my district.' Some 'very responsible members of the Chamber of Commerce' had asked him if it didn't make sense to decriminalize pot. Would it not 'diversify the economy, broaden the tax base, and create jobs in this high-unemployment area?'"[27]

Whether or not the IRS could catch any more taxpayers is debatable, but the Counter-Economy is already diversified and creating plenty of jobs, not only without government intervention but in spite and in defiance of it.

And, as always, we see the Capital Pyramid and the horizontal networking of the CounterEconomy, as exemplified by the drug market. "Marijuana is not merely a good crop. 'It's sent land values skyrocketing,' says realtor Roy Johnson. 'It's not my job to fink to the Internal Revenue Service, to ask where these guys get their money. Hell, it would be discrimination if I refused to sell them land.' So, in Garberville, there are more real estate offices than saloons on the main street."[28]

One politician seems to be ready for another Prohibition-surrender of 1933 in the Drug Wars. "Mendocino County's agricultural commissioner, Ted Eriksen Jr., recognized the industry's status by listing county production last year at $90 million. A higher authority ordered the entry deleted. Amiable, easy-going Eriksen, whose forebears have lived here since the turn of the century, says: 'I guess it's one thing to make money from moonshine, another to advertise the fact. Back in Prohibition days my daddy used to ship wine grapes out of the state in a box labeled DON'T CRUSH THIS. IT MIGHT TURN INTO WINE. I just don't see much difference in what's happening today. Pot is this county's No. 1 agricultural product. This harvest, it'll bring in more than $100 million. People who refuse to recognize that are burying their heads in the sand."[29]

Fortunately for those who wish to see the market untaxed, unregulated, and counter-economic, the Holy Warrior hawks against drugs shall smite such compromising, realistic doves: "Next year [1982] is election year in California, so ambitious state politicians don't quite see it Eriksen's way. Attorney-General

George Deukmejian, running for governor, wants the commissioner fired and is taking court action to remove him."[30]

California is high-tech and technology comes in near the top of the Capital Pyramid. "Thanks to the curious sex life of cannabis sativa, California's young marijuana millionaires have been able to develop a strain of the weed that outclasses Colombian, Mexican, and even such specialties as Hawaii's fabled Maui Wowie in potency and popularity. Cultivation today calls for both science and tender loving care. It involves force feeding with fertilizer, chemical and organic, and above all 'selective breeding' — the systematic removal of male plants from the neighborhood of the female. Deprived of male companionship, the ungerminated heads of the female plant ooze a dark resin that contains 10 to 12 times as much tetrahydrocannabinol (THC) as do other varieties. THC is the active agent that gives smokers their high.

"The result is sinsemilla — literally, 'without seeds' — the most powerful strain of grass in the world, priced at $1,500 to $3,000 a pound, selling on the street for $200 an ounce."[31]

The Drug Warriors strike from the sky with liquid death — and the Counter-Economy simply accounts for the attack. "Helping to force up the price is the success of Mexico's paraquat spraying program, urged by the United States. Once it seemed that nearly every bag of 'weed' sold was purportedly Mexico's Acapulco gold. Today, the great fields south of the U.S. border are devastated annually with pesticides, and Mexico's share of the U.S. marijuana market has fallen to an estimated 10 per cent."[32]

Could not the Holy Spraying Inquisition hit the home-grown heretics? "Now some California legislators want to use paraquat on the northern plots. 'Why should the taxpayer pay for armies of drug enforcement agents to go in there and seize the stuff when paraquat could do the job quickly and easily?' asks Los Angeles Police Chief Daryl Gates.

"The answer is that growers, with heavy popular support, are taking an over-our-dead-bodies stand against spraying (which kills forest underbrush as well as pot plants). They helped push through a local ordinance that forbids aerial spraying, then handed frustrated police another setback when one county voted against accepting a federal grant to help pay for a 'sinsemilla strike force' set up by California's attorney-general."[33]

Most counter-economists don't stoop to politics for their risk-lowering. "Many farmers try to avoid risks and cut costs by planting on other people's land. National parks — where vast forest stretches off the beaten track rarely see a tourist — and other federal properties are much favored. Says one narcotics agent in Ukiah, the county's seat, 'We've found farms in a dozen national forests, at Big Sur, even on the Hunter-Ligett Military Reservation (a huge military training ground).' Others simply grow it in their own backyard. A 55-year-old grandmother, Jane Schimpff, recently arrested with a crop worth $50,000, said she had grown her 60 plants as 'a hedge against inflation.'"[34]

More on inflation eounter-economics next chapter. But Ms. Schimpff's action is quintessentially counter-economic, whatever the market. "Had she known her plantation was so valuable, 'Why heavens, I'd have covered it up better.'"[35] Surely. And her associates know this well and live by it.

"Two years ago Attorney General Deukmejian launched an all-out war on the farms, leading his agents personally into the fray, followed by TV crews. Armed with helicopters and an array of electronic warfare gadgets the strike force seized and destroyed tonnes of weed worth millions of dollars.

"But despite the huge hauls, agents say they probably seize less than 10 per cent of what is grown in this area."[36] Where have we heard this before?

By the way, Florida is not so innocent of dope agriculture anymore. "An aerial survey has uncovered at least 155 marijuana fields in 41 north and central Florida counties, the authorities reported yesterday. Federal and State agents have seized 51,189 plants since the surveying project began June 1, the Florida Department of Law Enforcement said. The clandestine fields included one in Levy County that contained 13,500 marijuana plants up to 12 feet tall."[37]

The Network

It does not matter which way the State goes in the near future. Should it legalize "grass," "coke" and "dust" and "horse" will take up the slack in the labs and distribution nets and farmers will "rotate their crops." Some marginal producers will move out, maybe into tax-evasion counseling. On the other hand, should the State prohibit something new — thousands of drugs are discovered every year — or old, like tobacco, the market will expand, and a few more marginal cases who were thinking about growing, trucking, or dealing will enter. The State cannot win — though some statists, making a career out of the Drug Menace, can. And the Counter-Economy cannot lose, though the poor risks will get weeded out by arrests. And the Capital Pyramid keeps growing with new technology and techniques.

The drug market reminds us of what we have seen in the Soviet Union, much as that may irk anti-communists who enjoyed that section. Perhaps it will help them to accept it if they realize that a Red takeover of the U.S. would find an intact Counter-Economy ready to spread out into newly-controlled fields.

Two concepts introduced in this chapter will be referred to heavily for the rest of the book: the Capital Pyramid and the horizontal network. Before we leave drugs, the latter lesson has yet to be absorbed in fullness. Let us walk up the side of the Capital Pyramid and see just how much this one sector of the Counter-Economy touches lives (we noted a similar phenomenon in Chapter One, you may recall).

First, the consumers at our base. Every family's got one or more, even remote Utah Mormon communities or withdrawn Brooklyn Hassidic neighborhoods. No point in belaboring this save to note that every person who knows of a family member using any illicit substance is guilty of conspiracy. That is, they're the "organized" part of organized crime without even touching anything illegal. (Who said we don't have Thought Police yet?) At this point, nearly the entire population of North America is involved already.

But every dealer has friends, relatives, and acquaintances who "cover" for him or her, perhaps provide him with safe places and stashes — maybe a college dorm roommate, maybe a fraternity brother or sorority sister. And there are the people in the street or campus quad or Malibu cocktail party who see the transactions and let it happen, perhaps even spontaneously warning the entrepreneur of the passage of law enforcement.

This libertarian network, which some might consider an entangling web of corruption, spreads through the rural farming communities as farmers or their hip offspring diversify the crops blackly. Scientific labs get a little moonlighting action and silent lab assistants and cooperative technicians join the network without membership cards.

"Federal drug enforcers are 'falling behind' in the fight against secret laboratories in this country that illegally produce stimulants, depressants, and hallucinogens, congressional investigators said Friday. The General Accounting Office said in a report that these non-narcotic, dangerous drugs killed more than 3,200 persons in 1979 — more than five times the number killed by heroin, the drug enforcers' primary target. Most of the synthetic drugs are produced in clandestine laboratories or diverted from the legitimate drug distribution systems the report said.

"A few DEA field offices have achieved 'an impressive increase' in the number of secret lab seizures — from 33 in 1975 to 234 in 1980 — but the illicit labs continue to flourish, the report said."[38]

Garages may find they're providing and repairing a lot of vehicles paid for in kilos rather than dollars Or at least in cash; in any event, you don't fill out any papers on their jobs and don't ask why they have hollow bumpers or hidden doors. Hangar techs at airfields and dock workers at yachting marinas find silence may be Acapulco golden. And then there's their families and friends who find out, accidentally or casually, where that bonus came from and, rather than report it promptly as required by law, they join the network.

At the top of the Capital Pyramid, we may well find the network extends out from bankers who know where their big depositors came from but — officially — not their money... and their family and friends at the country club and social register, including campaign donors, lawyers... and judges. At this point, vested interest seems an appropriate term for the strands linking the network.

142

Up and down, spread out across all of society, from bohemian artists to research chemists, from skid row to the boardroom, and from Watts to Beverly Hills, the network grows, losing a few leaves, branches and roots, but always sprouting more. The affinities and confidence that fill out this skeletal structure may be extended to tax resistance, draft evasion, inflation protection (next chapter), and all the other forms of Counter-Economics this book covers.

Often Drug Counter-Economics is the first contact Western youth has with what their Eastern counterparts contact from birth (and with the Home Birth movement — see Chapter Thirteen — that may change, too) the "left-hand goods." Nalevo. It is a lesson that will serve them well as they run into network after network in the market that really serves the world: the CounterEconomy.

"America's appetite for marijuana appears insatiable. At least 11 tonnes a day go up in smoke, and consumers demand ever more potent Strains of the drug. Former White House adviser and drug authority Dr. Peter Bourne estimates that the marijuana industry is among the top halfdozen money-makers in the nation, totaling around $50 billion. Bourne, an advocate of smaller penalties for possession (but not of legalization), calls marijuana 'the country's most difficult drug problem, a politician's nightmare.'"[39] And a counter-economist's delight.

One problem that these networks have is a problem in using money; that is, using the State's monopoly currency. "Four million dollars, in small bills, is a bit like a St. Bernard: nice, but hard to hide. So when federal agents burst into the office of a Miami drug ring last August, they found a pile of money the size of a small refrigerator. The $4-million haul represented two days' cash flow for a smuggling operation, posing as a currency exchange firm, that authorities said had been operating in south Florida for 15 months. The bust represents a new emphasis on an old law-enforcement tool — catch crooks by tracking their profits. Few drug dealers accept MasterCard or Visa, so wholesalers quickly accumulate boxes, bags, and suitcases full of 10- and 20-dollar bills.

"'It's a very severe logistical problem for criminals to move that much cash,' says William Meglen, director of the Custom Service's currency investigation division. 'I mean, we're talking bulk.'"[40]

143

But the Counter-Economy is nothing if not innovative and ingenious. "Frustrated criminals sometimes try to transfer the money in unusual ways. Maria Rojas of Bogota, Colombia, was arrested at the Miami airport last year carrying $1.5 million in eight 'factory-sealed' Monopoly boxes. In Florida, stories of customers paying for luxury automobiles with shopping bags of money are common. One suspected cocaine dealer paid cash for various parcels of real estate, a Rolls-Royce, and a 60-foot yacht.

"Miami has become well-known as the Wall Street of this underground cash. Federal authorities point to what they call the 'grotesque' amount of currency flowing into the Miami Federal Reserve Bank — where deposits jumped from around $471 million in 1974 to over $4 billion in 1979."[41]

What the substance-of-your-choice vendors need to learn is what our tax rebels are learning: how to get out of the State's money system, at least partially. And an additional reason, which they all share with the rest of the economy, is the State's depreciation of the forced medium of exchange — inflation.

And so, as we have come to expect, the market responds with inflation Counter-Economics.

Footnotes

1. The author (SEK3) is particularly indebted to the famous psychiatrist Dr. Thomas
Review) for stimulating his evolution but he is responsible for his own views. For those checking on vested interests, the author confesses to be a social drinker and pipe smoker. This area is one of my rare cases of moderation.
2. Böhm-Bawerk, E. V. (1890) Capital and interest. New York: Macmillan & Co. We'll be seeing more of the Austrians all through the book.

3. The marijuana smuggling war is heating up the high seas. (1981, January 5). Zodiac News Service.
4. McReynolds, M. (1981, September 7). Uphill fight against trafficking — Colombia coast region a 'pot' empire. Los Angeles Times, p. IA-10.

5. Ibid.

6. Ibid.

7. Ibid.

8. Ibid.

9. Ibid.

10. Ibid.

11. Kennedy, J. M. (1981, October 17). "Petroleum of Lebanon" goes to market: Hashish harvest is a profitable fact of life in war-torn country. Los Angeles Times, p. IA-1.

12. Ibid.

13. Ibid.

14. Ibid.

15. Ibid.

16. Ibid.

17. Ibid.

18. Pakistan opium flooding west. (1981, October 11). Los Angeles Times, p. I-5.

19. Ibid.

20. Ibid.

21. Ibid.

22. Ibid.

23. Federal officials say that the state of Florida would suffer…. (1980, April 14). Zodiac News Service.

24. The author had personal contact with an agent of this futures market in 1975 but it has passed into other hands since.

25. Scobie, W. (1981, October 12). Pot luck in the high hills. Maclean's 94(41), p. 11.

26. Ibid.

27. Ibid.

28. Ibid.

29. Ibid., p. 14.

30. Ibid.

31. Ibid.

32. Ibid.

33. Ibid., p. 17.

34. Ibid.

35. Ibid.

36. Ibid.

37. 155 marijuana fields found in aerial survey of Florida. (1981, November 17). New York Times, p. 12.

38. Ostrow, R. J. (1981, November 14). Drug agents face overdose of secret labs: GAO accuses enforcers of losing battle against non-narcotics. Los Angeles Times, p. I-10.

39. Scobie, W. op. cit., p. 11.

40. Grier, P. (1981, October 29). Paperwork used to do in drug dealers: Profits traced as federal agents press drive against cash-laden criminals. Los Angeles Times, p. IC-1.

41. Ibid.

5. Inflation Counter-Economics

Inflation: The Great Counter-Economizer

Inflation connects and interacts with all of Counter-Economics from taxes to drugs (as we have just seen and will see more of presently) and beyond. Its effects, and the recent attempts to comprehend its nature and workings, have been a great radicalizer of North Americans. Europeans of East and West and Third Worlders have been as much if not more affected by inflation, and taken counter-economic measures against it (most spectacularly in Poland and the most inflationary Latin American countries) but consciousness-raising there has not matched that of North America, where an entire genre of non-fiction books emerged in the early nineteenseventies predicting further, more catastrophic inflation, advising measures to be taken against economic ruin (mostly practical measures for individuals and families) and, most spectacularly, anticipating correctly the surge in gold price.

Inflation touches — or contaminates — so much of economics (and counter–economics) because money is involved in most transactions in a developed economy. The exceptions are easily listed: "psychic" profit of emotional gain and barter. But even many things — if not most — done for love involve costs in goods and services, and "above-ground" bartering is far more expensive than the equivalent market transaction with some form of money. (Counter-economic bartering is another concept entirely, as will soon be shown.)[1]

The shock of sudden awareness of an inflation victim who discovers what money is and how his or her government manipulates it compares closely to that of a comfortable patriot facing a draft notice and discovering that this war is meaningless. Or the shock of a conservative businessman finding out that the taxes which will destroy him not only were justified by his beloved Constitution but that the Federalist government first organized under the Constitution promptly crushed the Pennsylvania Whisky Tax rebels.

Yet war and taxes are often lightly felt by some victims and harshly by others. Inflation is the great counter-economizer: it plunders all without favor — though, it should be stressed, that plunder goes somewhere to someone. Widows, orphans, the handicapped, and the devout religious retreatists are exempt from war and taxes — but not inflation.

The very study of Counter-Economics and its development by this author began with the great Gold Bug Wave of 1972-73. Harry Browne in particular, along with Harry Schultz, and later Douglas Casey and John Pugsley and many others, took a long step from the old free-enterprise economic movement largely identified with the political Right. Where these anti-inflation activists departed from conservatives was by advocating and demonstrating where individuals could take concrete actions to opt-out of the general economy and protect themselves. Conservative free-enterprisers continued to urge support of a different government which would roll back the State through any of the political parties: Democrats, Republicans, Libertarians; even the leftist Peace and Freedom Party was considered as the vehicle for a time (1974).

Harry Browne took yet another step beyond the How You Can Prosper From The Coming Collapse genre with his How I Found Freedom In An Unfree World. Browne discovered
loopholes in the State's network of regulations not just in inflation-protection but throughout the market. That is, one could legally — or at least not illegally — evade all taxation, inflation, and controls. Of course, this freedom had a high price in an unfree world.

The flaws in Browne's positions discouraged some of his large readership but encouraged others to take the next step. One of the flaws of Browne's living-inthe-interstices was that one was forced to go where the State inadvertently directed. There was a further risk involved in that the government could change its mind and clamp down — and usually would as soon as someone (like Browne) made these interstices public and popular.

And so the final step was taken by this author and a few others in 1973: why not apply the lessons of evading the State's regulations and controls to evading the State's enforcement of controls? To the surprise of most of us, we theoretical types found a fully flourishing market already there — without awareness of why they should be doing what they were doing.

Gold was the catalyst and that was no accident. Several libertarians who were involved in smuggling gold and then publicly displaying it, defying the American States to arrest them and give them a test case, found that they were left largely unbothered. The idea expanded: if the State was largely impotent to suppress gold when it was illegal, then what was really stopping us from replacing the paper money of the United States with gold — at least in *our* transactions?

And so it came to pass that a gold bank (under an assumed name, of course) developed and is flourishing today. But to grasp the implications of this event and just how apocalyptic it is, Counter-Economics is going to have to review a little basic economics.

The Nature of Inflation

The word inflation is used in two ways, which adds to the considerable confusion on the subject. Most often, it conjures up rising prices. The original and proper definition is much clearer and will be used here. Inflation is the increase of a fiat (government-created) money supply. One of its consequences is a general increase in prices (though individual prices can go counter to the trend).

Money is a medium of exchange. As many who have experimented with the recent bartering fad have discovered, having something popular to trade, or to trade for, greatly facilitates finding trading partners. Someone may want your oil paintings very much but you need shoes, not the music concert they're offering. Maybe a shoemaker likes music enough…? If half the trading partners smoke, tobacco will (and often does) become a medium of exchange. Even non-smokers will accept it, knowing plenty of smokers to trade with.

People historically went through several different media of exchange. The more universally accepted the commodity was, the better money it made. Durability was useful for savings; who wanted their nest egg to spoil? And such things as easy divisibility for change, compactness, and consistency of quality all enhanced the monetary aspect. For good solid chemical reasons, one substance became the obvious and unique choice — and its closest cousins in the chemist's periodic table of the elements were the favored alternatives.

Gold, silver, copper, platinum, and palladium — these are the material forms chosen to embody the highly useful abstraction of money. In French, the word for money is silver (argent). Gold is synonymous with money in Danish (geld). Pounds sterling were pounds of silver, even the dollar defined a (Spanish) measure of precious metal.

Fiat money is money imposed by the State. Sometimes the king merely ratified the prevailing currency and was satisfied to put his royal or imperial likeness on a measure of coined precious metal to "guarantee" its value. Actually, the value was rubbing off in the other direction; how many rulers were as "good as gold?"

Rather than guaranteeing the value, beginning at least in the Roman Empire, the rulers debased the coins by alloying with base metals or "clipping" the edges of the coin so that less-thanexpected weight (mass, actually, for the sake of purity) was tendered in exchange. Without going over the long history of money in detail, it is fair to say that the relationship between State and money is corruption and fraud. If money is the root of evil, the root of evil money is government.[2]

Fiat money is money imposed by fiat. It is neither voluntary nor spontaneously generated in free trading between consenting adults. The United States alone has had several severe inflation bouts through fiat money, beginning with the "Continentals" of the Revolution. There is also a strong link between war and inflation: the Continentals, the Greenbacks of the Civil War/War Between The States, severe inflation of World Wars I and II, Korea, and Viet Nam. This is not a coincidence, Inflation is a form of taxation and fighting wars needs lots of taxes.

Like taxation, inflation must be enforced. The mechanism of imposition of fiat money is the legal-tender law. One must accept the debased government paper certificates allegedly representing money or face legal penalty.

In Nationalist China, just before the collapse of its control over the mainland, the inflation of currency was so severe (to finance the Chinese Civil War) that merchants defying the monetary and price controls were lined up and shot by officials of Generalissimo Chiang Kai-Shek. Mao Tse-Tung promised gold and won over the small "capitalists" to his Communist regime.[3]

150

If traders would risk death rather than take inflated fiat money, then the link between hyperinflation and revolution (or at least drastic changes in government) is not coincidental. Failing a general upheaval, the Counter-Economy is strongly stimulated by strong inflation. (Price controls, often used to combat inflation — like holding down the mercury in a thermometer to combat fever — turn almost the entire market into a black market overnight.) Gold hoarding is common among even poor people in European and Latin American countries with repeated bouts of hyperinflation.

North Americans are the most complacent people on the globe about accepting fiat money as real money. One of the reasons is that the last collapse of the currency was two hundred years ago in the U.S. But the current escalating debasement of the American dollar is shaking that trust and the flight to legal gold, foreign assets and foreign currency, and counter-economic substitutes is accelerating.

Although there are a few secondary factors (which can be mostly eliminated by long-term averaging), the "price of gold" has not gone drastically up. Gold is the most stable medium of exchange possible. The price of the dollar in terms of gold has dropped drastically. In terms of the original gold weight definition of the dollar (used throughout the prosperous, mostly hardmoney century from 1814-1914), today's dollar is worth three cents to a nickel. If any of you remember that at the turn of the century a beer with a free lunch cost four cents, you can see the price ratio is still in line.

It is fairly obvious that if people are free to choose their own money as some economists have recently suggested[4] — that is, people are free to refuse one form of money and contract for payment in another — then either the government will behave itself and simply superfluously certify the measure of the money (which can always be checked by physical and chemical means) or government money will be discounted and Gresham's Law will take over.

Gresham's Law has usually been stated as "bad money drives out good." (The "good" money is being hoarded and the "bad money" is given in payment and thus predominates in circulation.) This ends with the "Crack-Up Boom" when the "bad money" is worthless and only "good money" is left.

The nature of inflation, then, is that it is a form of theft by the rulers of a country. The money supply is first controlled by the government, and then the State increases the number of units by various bookkeeping manipulations.

More dollars chasing the same amount of goods is inflation in a nutshell. It does have other effects, but, save for a privileged few, they are overwhelmingly negative to most values of most people. In order to realize the apocalyptic nature of inflation and the growingly countereconomic survival movement, a quick sketch of the long-range, cataclysmic effects are needed.

Inflation and Survivalism

Inflation causes depressions; depressions motivate greater inflation. The spiral repeats until a critical point at which the money system collapses — the "Crack-Up Boom" of Ludwig Von Mises. A recent dramatic example was Germany in 1923. The discrediting of the governing political parties led to the National Socialist takeover and the Third Reich, an event most would consider cataclysmic.

It seems paradoxical that many apparently level-headed investment advisors, market analysts, gold bugs, and such are heavily committed to "end of the world" doom 'n' gloom scenarios. The above sketch explains why.[5]

Survivalists see a general, world-wide runaway inflation and collapse of the money supply. Extrapolating present conditions along historically verified economic lines proves them right. And so they store gold, silver, and commodities in out-of-the-way foreign places or in the North American wilderness.

The Survivalists are often willing to evade and break laws and controls. After all, if the end of the world is coming — and the government is responsible — why should the State be obeyed? And so they take the step into the Counter-Economy.

Typical counter-economic acts by Survivalists are tax evasion (of course), currency-control evasion (to store their money safely and undisclosed in foreign banks), building-regulation evasion (for survival retreats), gun-control evasion and drug-control evasion (to stock their retreats), contraband smuggling (if they wish a foreign retreat), and evasion of all compulsory disclosure laws. This last one is necessary; if the government can reach you, your money, and/or your survival retreat when the crunch comes, what good were your preparations? No survival results.

By laying in gold and goods — and even the poor can do it[6] — the move to a counter-economic money system was facilitated. It only took someone to realize that one need not wait for the eventual collapse to replace the money that the gold bugs and survivalists (now in the millions), at least, realized was forcibly imposed, intentionally debased, and far less preferable to top commodity alternatives. And so the Gold Bank was introduced. And since some of its operations — even with Browne's intersticing — skirt the laws, and all of them will be declared illegal when the inflation goes runaway (judging by most historical accounts), the Gold Bank must be counter-economic. And it is.

There is always the possibility that the government will come to its senses and stop inflating. That hope was, at least for North America, crushed by the election and "sell-out" of Ronald Reagan as president, generally considered the hardest "hard money" advocate who could possibly get elected to power. His Gold Commission refused to back a gold standard for the American dollar, and, as this is penned, the money supply of the United States is being pumped up for the next, higher than ever, turn of the spiral. The demoralization of the moderate gold bugs may actually be enough to set off the flight into real goods at this cycle. (See footnote 5.)

It may surprise some to find that the Counter-Economy actually offers considerable hope. The money supply could be replaced — illegally but peacefully — before the severest dislocations of the Crack-Up Boom. How it is being done (and how you can participate) will be spelled out from the real-life example after one last preliminary.

Counter-Economic Money

153

Ordinary people need protection against inflation. It hits everyone (no one can actually obey all laws since many contradict each other). Counter-economists (those described in previous chapters and following chapters) need a safe currency. What does that mean?

"A banker and three others were convicted Tuesday of participating in a scheme to launder drug money through Garfield Bank.... A federal jury deliberated less than two days before finding the four guilty of conspiracy and failure to comply with laws requiring banks to file reports on deposits of more than $10,000."[7]

All counter-economists need ways of conducting financial transactions free from the prying eyes of government in order to lower their risks considerably. In order to evade income disclosure, most are tax evaders as well. Some solve the problem by buying banks.

"John A. Gabriel, a former president of the [Garfield] bank and chairman of the board, was indicted along with the others in July. He pleaded guilty on charges of failing to report nearly $500,000 in currency transactions. Gabriel and the bank have paid the government nearly $2.3 million in fines."[8]

Owning a fiat bank operating counter-economically is useful, but not much more risky than operating a gold bank. Gold also has the advantage to drug dealers, smugglers, and all sorts of foreign-operating counter-economists, of being a far more universal medium of exchange than even the dollar.

"Black market gold in Moscow now brings prices equivalent to $2,400 an ounce — close to four times more than current world rates, according to sources familiar with the trade. In other parts of the country, such as Soviet Central Asia, prices are reputed to be even higher."[9]

Soviet fiat money is the most rigidly controlled. Is the ruble inflating? "Inflation also hits the black market. One source said a five-ruble Czarist gold coin that cost the equivalent of $100 on the black market in the 1960s now goes for close to $400. Even gold tooth fillings can be unloaded at premium prices."[10]

In other words, all the reasons for counter-economic money in North America applies to darkest Russia. "People who have acquired money illegitimately are understandably reluctant to put large sums in state-controlled banks for fear of unpleasant questions. Keeping huge stores of money at home is also dangerous. Since the 1917 Bolshevik revolution, the national currency has been changed several times — with the 'old money' becoming worthless after every reform...."

"'Anyone who doesn't want to have to account for how he got his money might well tend to put his money into gold,' said a Moscow writer who asked not to be identified. 'That way, it's always safe'... The black market offers no-questions-asked confidentiality."[11]

The collapse of Cambodia shows both the universality of gold and its function of redeemer during economic collapse. "Despite a ban by Thailand on cross-border trade, the river of gold that began flowing from Cambodia in 1979 with the first wave of starving refugees continues, fueling a black market that distributes scarce goods across Vietnamese-run Cambodia and pumps millions of dollars into the Thai economy. 'Business is better than ever,' one Cambodia trader said of the unofficial 'metals market' operating at Nong Chan, one of several unofficial refugee settlements straddling the border."[12]

The relationship between risk and profits — the basis of Counter-Economics — is starkly visible from the relation between gold price and distance (to perceived danger). "At tiny stalls in Nong Chan and similar border camps, such goods as soap, flashlight batteries, pens, and rice sell for only slightly more than they do at the nearby Thai market-town of Aranyaprathet. As the goods travel deeper into Cambodia, the prices rise accordingly, observers said...."

"'It's a dangerous trip back (into Cambodia) so these people want a good rate of return,' [one Western diplomat] said, adding that some of the goods actually find their way to Vietnam."[13] Perhaps the Counter-Economy has its own version of revenge.

Earlier it was put forth that inflation is a good consciousness raiser — or counter-economizer. How about the monetary-collapse-caused black market of Thailand ? (We know the Cambodians are radicalized.)

155

"Thai government efforts to stop the black market have angered Thai villagers, who say the trade is as active as ever but is reserved for the military. 'If you go to the border to sell to the Cambodians and the soldiers take your things, sell them and pocket the money in front of you, how can you feel?' one Thai trader asked. 'Before the black market, people liked the soldiers,' he said. 'Now 90% of the people fear and dislike them.'"[14]

Even with all this gold, banks are used. "...the diplomat said recent daily fund transfers from Aranyaprathet to Bangkok at one Thai bank had risen from a pittance before 1979 to $500,000."[15] One needs banks for two reasons: conveniently to handle large sums of wealth and to interface with the above-ground or white market.

Actually, there are other ways of handling large wealth counter-economically. Drugs such as cocaine and gems are easy to smuggle and conceal. The interface with the rest of the market is far more valuable to most large-scale counter-economists. The rich ones simply bribe their way into seemingly legitimate banks.

So what does the poorer and middle-class counter-economist do?

Convenient Gold

Fences, money-changers, and other middlemen have dealt with the problem of "laundering" black money into white. When money itself is the problem, one needs to keep most of one's money black (in illegal or soon-to-be-illegal hard money). One can sit on contraband goods, taking the additional risk, and converting one's assets when the time comes. Many survivalists find that fits nicely into their plans.

Suppose you could deposit fiat money in what appears to be a bank. This counter-economic bank converts your deposit into gold and holds the deposit in gold, safe from government ravages. Got a bill to pay? Write out a "check" and the Counter-Economic Gold Bank (C-EGB henceforth) turns gold into dollars at today's price and sends along an ordinary bank check with your paperwork. Got a counter-economic bill to pay? Write out a gold check to your trading partner who can collect gold from the C-EGB or have it deposited to their gold account without going through dollars at all or having any external evidence of transaction.

Such a description is not only a full counter-economist's dream but that of any part-time retreatist, survivalist, gold bug, or even inflation-ravaged widows and orphans. It's here already, at least in ahead-of-its-time Southern California.

The Counter-Economic Bank

The Counter-Economic Gold Bank is an honest-to-God innovation. Many, if not all, of those designated "the world's oldest profession" are counter-economic, but C-EGB is really something new. The rise of Information Counter-Economics has something to do with it, but to a large extent it owes its existence to greater understanding of economic theory combined with counter-economic action (see last three chapters).

Banks — or even near-banks — are tricky to get going. Confidence and trust must be earned, painfully and slowly. Since the consciousness increase of 1972, several have tried and failed. One, however, has succeeded and after 16 years of continuous operation is now the financial center of several "free-market businesses" including printers, typesetters, leather goods manufacturers, computer consultants, and several new businesses starting up at any time. We will return to this "Agorist Community" near the end of the chapter and in more detail on its operation near the end of the book.

This particular Counter-Economic Gold Bank will be called A&Co. Because of the laws concerning bank chartering (the government keeps tight rein on banks), A&Co. never calls itself a bank in its introductory literature but simply refers to itself as "A Free Market Business Trust" and operates openly but not obtrusively.

A&Co's main explanatory booklet of its operation has some euphemisms but straightforwardly calls the book Current Gold Accounts: A Free Market Money Instrument. After two pages of introductory economics of inflation, Current Gold Accounts gets right down to specifics. Money is defined in grams of gold (one troy ounce equals 31.10 grams). Up front, A&Co wants a contract signed with the account holder.

The mechanics are simple and precise. "The deposit-payment exchange rates for current gold accounts are:

• currently determined once a day, when gold markets are open, at 1:45 P.M. When our volume permits, we'll determine the rates more often during each business day;

• maintained at a 1% spread and

• based on the lowest premium gold coin available, which sometimes produces deposit rates at a discount from gold bullion and payment rates at a premium over gold bullion.

"Current gold accounts presently earn 1.0% pa [per annum], payable monthly, on balances between 100 grams Au (Au is the chemical symbol for gold) and 400-gms Au; amounts over 400 gms-Au do not earn interest at this time."

A&Co explains they accept deposits in gold pieces, federal reserve notes (dollars), postal money orders, and "dollar instruments (bank checks, money orders and so forth)." A of A&Co and others have personal checking accounts (they explain freely) to deal with the instruments.

Deposit slips are simple and one can either fill out gold directly in grams (if that is what is what is deposited) or in dollars and A&Co will insert the exchange rate, convert the dollars to gold grams, and send you your receipt with the final figures.

Gold may be deposited in any form. Gold will be paid out on demand in Austrian 100 Corona coins (30.5 gm). Since it is difficult to get "small change" in gold, one of the obvious advantages of a C-EGB is to poorer people who can now "speculate" in gold by depositing it in an A&Co account in dollars for conversion, and converting it back at a later price and time. Any and all dollars are acceptable.

(In case it is not yet obvious, paper money benefits the rich with government connections. Gold is the primary defense of the powerless poor. Long-standing propaganda to the contrary is clearly self-serving to certain interests. It is strongly in the interests of the rich and powerful beneficiaries of inflation to make gold difficult to obtain and transact.)

By the eighth page of Current Gold Accounts we are half-way through and the most complicated procedure is explained. The checks of the gold bank itself are called "transfer orders" and one may write one to another member of the bank to transfer either gold or dollars. The only complication is, as was mentioned in the previous section, in transferring payment to the "outside market," that is, interfacing. A&Co, quite reasonably to gain consumer interest, undertakes the effort involved. One sends A&Co the transfer order and bill and they send out an ordinary, regular-bank check with your paperwork.

"When sending instructions to us to make payments from your gold account, include:

• an invoice, bill or some other form of explanation of the payment,

• a transfer order for each payee with full instructions, such as name of payee, amount of payment and form of payment if different from commercial bank check and

• an unsealed envelope stamped and addressed to payee.

"If any of these items is missing, we'll still process the payment but charge a reasonable fee for the extra handling."

What could be simpler? Examples are then given, including the gold-to-dollar calculations. A&Co points out that it may take them one to three days to handle the more complex transactions. It is next noted that accounts are turned over once a month (usual for most banking type operations).

The remainder of this simple booklet gives examples of procedures, sample calculations, and a list of benefits. One benefit is avoiding capital gains penalties for those reporting income. This deserves a little more coverage. If one has bought 20 grams of gold for $200 and later sells it for $400 to pay some debt, one could (if reporting it) end up paying taxes on the gain of $200. But since the dollar declined to half its value in reality rather than gold doubling its value, one actually preserved one's wealth, nothing more. Yet one will still be liable for taxes on this illusory capital gain. Although hard-core counter-economists would not report themselves to taxing powers, soft-core or grey-market counter-economists might wish to "cover themselves." A&Co gives a service, then, to these halfway people as well.

Privacy is another benefit with obvious counter-economic implications. A&Co also mentions their minimal charges, paying interest in gold, and having a simple way to buy gold without the high premiums charged by coin dealers for small purchases. Characteristically, the last benefit they mention is "support of the free market."

A regular newsletter issued by A&Co is the Free Market Advertiser, which publishes the gold/dollar exchange rates they use over a month, publicizes associated counter-economic businesses, and publishes their reports to shareholders. A&Co also maintains a small stock exchange for these businesses.

These people know what they are doing and why. Economic and ideological articles and editorials on the virtues of the pure free market and attacks on the immorality of State taxation and regulation abound. Their consciousnesses have been raised.

Problems of the Counter-Economic Bank

Many will find it amazing that something as organized and sophisticated as a bank (not to mention embryonic stock exchange) can operate as if in anarchy — with no government. The high probity of the principals of A&Co — non-smoking, non-drinking, and so on — certainly belies the black-market image, yet they do not discriminate against "looser" countereconomists.[16] As long as they add their bills properly and pay them, all are welcome. Needless to say, the bank is a main source of investment capital for local counter-economists.

A theme that should have been noticed already in this book is of the relative impotence of government. Law-enforcement is helpless in even the most totalitarian dictatorship when laws are not strongly accepted and enforced on people by themselves. Even when everyone — including counter-economists — agrees with the wrongfulness of an act (such as murder or theft), the State's own statistics of apprehension hit a high of only about 20%. (That is, over 80% of true criminals in the worst crimes get away from the inefficient government apparatus.)

One important factor in minimizing the risk of state interference in one's activities is the tacit or stronger support of everyone involved. In the case of the Counter-Economic Gold Bank, it gives strong, continuous benefits to those with whom it does business. This is at least as important as ideological exhortations to remain loyal and the potential ostracism of one's trading partners and customers, should one report the activities to the State. Perhaps the State could offer a high enough reward to convince some to turn stool-pigeon but that has yet to happen after seven years and hundreds of people aware of the nature of the activities. And as this free market expands, the benefits involved in it grow, and the reward or bounty needs to get higher and higher until the State can no longer raise enough to crush a significant part at all.

A particularly sensitive problem for Inflation Counter-Economics, though common to all, is the flow and storage of information. Publicity and advertising is good for business; regular financial disclosure builds trust, confidence and more business, yet the more information about countereconomic activity is disclosed, the greater the risk that even Keystone Kops will accidentally trip across it, realize what is going on, and act to stop it.

Fortunately, at the same time that the counter-economy is getting more financially sophisticated, information technology is experiencing breakthroughs in storage and transmittal which are now completely free of unwanted intrusion.

The next chapter looks at the rise of Information Counter-Economics. If Inflation is the Great Counter-Economizer, then the Information industry explosion is the new shining, white-knight defender of the Counter-Economy.

Barter Counter-Economics

Bartering has become a recent fad and its motivation is largely tax avoidance and inflation evasion. A recent book actually claimed that openly trading without money was the new "underground" or "subterranean" economy. The truth is almost the opposite.

 Reported bartering is taxed. Most of the new, big, barter networks with computer accounting and high-profile advertising disclose their transactions to the Internal Revenue Service or its equivalent in other countries. The IRS assigns a value to the goods exchanged and demands taxes on the income. Sales tax may or may not be collected in the various localities and so on. Even where taxation is avoided in part, the governments at the appropriate level can pass new taxes on the transactions whenever they wish.

There are other advantages to open bartering such as those for cash-poor companies but as we have seen at least sketchily earlier in the chapter, the use of some form of money to mediate exchange is highly profitable. It is no accident that businesses keep discovering that they have barter credits, yet can't find what they need to purchase while many goods offered go untaken.

Counter-economic bartering has quite a different function. The current dollar (or gold or whatever) value of the goods are acknowledged by the trader and cash often changes hands surreptitiously to make change.

The Barter Book of 1979 spells out several straightforward rules for engaging in barter, all common-sense, but two in particular are blatantly counter-economic:

"They [barterers who are named] use direct exchange. They never get involved with third-party barter. They have heard of barter-credit systems and barter clubs, but they are not interested. If the premium were on efficiency, they would use money.

"They reap tax advantages. They do not record their loose, unstructured, friendly wages."[17]

Without high taxation and ever-higher inflation of paper money, the inconvenience and expense of abandoning the medium of exchange would quickly rule out bartering for most busy people. The 1981 "free-enterprise scare" of Ronald Reagan's election and early administration — with people anticipating (wrongly) a fall in taxes and inflation — caused barter exchanges to fail or suffer loss of customers. Vigorous, publicized IRS attacks on them quickly wiped them out.

Counter-economic bartering goes on but as a better way becomes apparent (gold-banking convenience) it will make way.

Still, even barter Counter-Economics would be immensely facilitated and approach the finetuning convenience of money-use with the introduction of computer nets. "Money is information" has already become a cliché. If everyone joined at least one computer network which linked with all the others, it would, at least in theory, work as fast and conveniently as using money. And the rise of Information Counter-Economics may allow just that.

Even in that ideal outcome, there would be no reason not to run the accounts in units of gold mass simply to include all the hold-outs and curmudgeons and those without computer hook-up or between such hook-ups.

Preliminary negotiations have begun with A&Co to issue the first counter-economic credit card (a Bank AnarchoCard ?). It is no coincidence that those offering the service are computer consultants and programmers.

Footnotes

1. A recent book, How To Prosper In The Underground Economy by Larry Burkett with William Proctor (William Morrow & Company 1982), completely misses this point. There is nothing "underground" — or at least counter-

economic — about barter dealings when books are open to the Internal Revenue Service.

2. A lot of literature has recently been published on the nature and history of money, from strident pamphlets to exact but opaque economic analyses. One of the most precise, easy, and enjoyable to read is still What Has Government Done To Our Money? by Dr. Murray N. Rothbard, a former student of Ludwig Von Mises and a rare economist not serving the interests of any government or would-be government.

3. As related to the author by Economist-Historian Professor Murray N. Rothbard, PhD.

4. Nobel-prize-winning Austrian economist Friedrich Von Hayek now suggests competing currencies be allowed and money "denationalized" by the State.

5. Most Austrian-economic-based writing has explained the business cycle in detail since the landmark publishing of Von Mises's doctoral thesis: Theory of Money And Credit (1910). It explained the Great Depression 19 years before it happened. Here's a longer sketch for those who wish to avoid looking up references: Increasing the money supply gives the first recipients in line (government rulers, banks, contractors with the government) more purchasing power. They bid up certain resources at the old prices and signal the producers to produce more because the producers think they can make more money. Eventually there is a general price rise, people find they can afford much less with the same money and cut back on their spending. Over-invested businesses that had increased production now get signals to reduce output, and liquidation ("fire sales" to "going out of business sales") and layoffs occur. This unemployment and capital loss is called a depression (or recession or other euphemism such as "rolling readjustment"). It could end there but the panicking bankrupt businessmen and unemployed laborers call for more money to solve the problem. The government obligingly prints more. But, to trick the market again into the first boom (or another like it), it has to print more than expected. (After all, everyone's already seen the prices rising, assume they will continue to rise at the same rate, and discount the money accordingly.) Eventually, the people catch on that they will be tricked again and anticipate any hike. At that point, the money is spent as fast as it is received (what Mises called the "flight into real goods"), workers are paid two or three times a day, debts have to be refinanced daily or even hourly. Finally, people throw away the worthless money to use foreign currencies, barter, and gold. This is the Crack Up Boom ending runaway

164

inflation. There are several historical examples of it and it sounds inevitable. Chile broke the cycle by means of a severe military dictatorship in 1973. For a fast-paced fictional account of a Crack-Up Boom in the United States in the near future, see Alongside Night by J. Neil Schulman (Ace Books, 1982; Crown 1979). Schulman is in full understanding of the theory of Counter-Economics (agorism) and his plot is resolved with the upbeat ending of agorist triumph.

6. See The Alpha Strategy by John Pugsley for useful details.

7. Morain, D. (1981, December 16). 4 guilty in money-laundering scheme. Los Angeles Times, p. II3.

8. Ibid.

9. Kent, T. (1980, September 4). Black market in gold thrives in Russia. Associated Press.

10. Ibid.

11. Ibid.

12. Wary gold dealers fuel black market: Thai sellers often dress in rags. (1982, January 10). Los Angeles Times, p. II-7.

13. Ibid.

14. Ibid.

15. Ibid.

16. Hargis, A. L. (1981). Current gold accounts: A free market money instrument. Costa Mesa, California: Anthony L. Hargis & Co., A Free Market Business Trust. Editor's Note: SEK3 obscured the name as "A&Co." at the time of writing to protect ALH&Co. from unwanted state interest. Alas, the activities of ALH&Co. came under scrutiny in 1996; in 2004 the company's assets (i.e., customers' gold and regular-bank deposits) were seized by the IRS. Anthony L. Hargis was imprisoned for contempt of court after refusing to turn over his records. See: Kristof, K. M. (2004, March 10). U.S. sues O.C. man in tax scam. Los Angeles Times. Retrieved from http://articles.latimes.com/2004/mar/10/business/fi-taxscam10.

17. Simon, D. A. (1979, October). Bartering: The tricks of the trade. Cosmopolitan, p. 226.

6. Information Counter-Economics

Information exchange divides the Counter-Economy from the Establishment white market. Consider the elementary difference between a street deal with and without the watchful eyes of State agents. Or consider a ship docking, unloading its goods, accepting payment, and sailing off. In one case, the forms were filled out and the imports registered with the government; in the identical case physically — but not informationally — no papers were filed with the State and its agents remained unaware of its existence. At the stroke of information exchange, contraband was created and the crime of smuggling occurred.

Control of information is a battle over the State's very ability to function. If you could cut off all information flow to the government, it would be unable to act. Strangely, the United States government recently threw in the towel over information-industry regulation. And yet conflict remains around the fringes, especially over the powerful computer programming method known as public key cryptography.

Should cryptography succeed, the long-awaited dream of workable anarchy has arrived. To understand the full impact, let us look at how the State works, or, rather, how it *steals*.

Plunder Through The Ages

In the beginning, the State was a gang of bandits, terrorizing the countryside. Taxation was simple; the horde seized anything that looked valuable, ate anything that looked edible, and raped anything that looked appealing. To beat the barbarians, the smart peasant hid his gold, his daughters (and sons), and his livestock. To discourage this cut-off of information, the horde often burned down the villages when they had taken all they could find.

Where the plunderers settled down to become a proper government, they restrained their appetites and exacted tribute that left the peasant with just enough to live on and grow another crop next year. Priests were bought to convince the producers that the State had divine approval. And by the Middle Ages the Lords settled for only the first night with the peasant bride (droit du seigneur)

166

The main form of tribute evasion remained underreporting of assets. But as the market grew more complex, some business activity underreported its very existence. The informer is looked on with greatest disdain and fear from the schoolyard to the prison yard. The "stool pigeon" receives an automatic death sentence from violent gangs (themselves embryonic states); nevertheless, informers are shunned by moral, peaceful counter-economists.

American society of the twentieth century is riddled with informers. Just to keep some perspective, anyone in the USSR not an informer is being informed on. And even the informers are informed on. One's safest course is to discover one's informer and then select their information carefully.

The drug industry is riddled with DEA and local police informers. Gun-runners run free until the BATF gets an informer in their midst. Political dissidents often have more dues-paying members from the Federal Bureau of Investigation than from committed members. The Federal Trade Commission depends on sore-loser competitors to denounce a company for anti-trust violations.

And above them all, with a network of spies, informers, disgruntled competitors, vengeful spouses, spurned lovers, and straight-out bounty hunters, stands the Internal Revenue Service. No legal agency of state enforcement excites the dread and fear as that of the IRS.

The IRS is the raised sword and mailed fist of the State. While the rest of the State camouflages itself with the appearance of good works, attempts to cosmeticize the taxman inevitably fall flat. A popular bumper sticker says it all: "IRS: It Really Steals."

How Taxation Works…

In the modern world, IRS agents cannot, much as they may wish, mount their sweat-soaked stallions, draw their morningstars and maces, and ride shrieking through the peaceful suburbs in search of wealth for the Director. Then again, they have an advantage over their spiritual ancestors of three millennia ago.

Their victims turn themselves in.

Three thousand years of mystification pay off every April 15 in the U.S. (April 30 in Canada, various spring days in other countries). American citizens are asked to send in the very information the State needs to know. The exact amount doesn't matter; the deductions are window-dressing.

The stark truth is that, without that volunteered information, the State would have no idea where the wealth is.

It is no new observation that if everyone stopped sending in their 1040 forms the State would dry up and blow away. The counter-economic insight is that anyone can (and does) do it without waiting for everyone else. The technique is to control the information flow about oneself; in particular, the information flow from you to the State.

Visibility and Profile

There is not just one way to use information to free one from State predation. There are three ways. Two of them assume you are acting relatively alone, the third assumes the opposite.

Most people are familiar with Low-Profile tactic of being "invisible" to the IRS and other government agencies. The rest of this chapter will focus on that method. What should not be forgotten are the other tactics, especially as they have higher payoffs (and correspondingly greater risks).

High-Profile Counter-Economics deals with a particular area of State coercion by calling attention to his or her victimization. The more noise, the better. The famed Chicago 8 used publicity to keep themselves out of prison for years — even after their convictions.

Civil disobedients trust public pressure to keep them out of jail or to minimize their penalties. Indeed, the State's enforcers are wary of creating martyrs. The very concept of martyr exhibits the power of Information; what is a martyr but a corpse with a good story?

High-Profile Counter-Economists have higher risks because they are so easy to detect. They gain the advantage of additional information flow — from themselves to the rest of the market. To the extent they succeed, they become inspirational.

Actually, this author has proven that it is possible to pursue the advantages of both High Profile and low visibility simultaneously. The trick was to create a third category: The CounterEconomic Community.

One may pursue any degree of notoriety (or, to put it another way, freely advertise one's services) within the community of fellow counter-economists while not informing the State, its agents, and, of course, its informers. To do that, one needs to control the flow of information about oneself.

Information Flow

Ever notice that after you order something by mail, or contribute to a charity or politician, your mailbox is suddenly flooded with associated solicitations? You have generated outward information flow and were rewarded by an inward torrent.

Information is the raw resource of a burgeoning industry, including data processing and much of computer programming. Information theory is a hot academic field. This is such a fast-changing business that the American government threw up its hands in its attempt to regulate it.[1]

Setting the discussion of higher technology to the side briefly, there are two obvious ways to escape the State's notice: don't exist; if you do exist, don't tell anyone about it. (There is also the agorist procedure: tell only fellow counter-economists who have as much to hide.)

Some counter-economists go that far. They cut themselves off from contact with anyone who might get to know them, get and stay off all mailing lists, operate through cash and never use banks, and even avoid legal residences, living in trailers as nomads or on neglected land in caves or makeshift structures.

Briefly, in the 1960s, these early self-conscious counter-economists (protoagorists, one might call them), were organized enough to publish a newsletter, Vonulife. (Vonu, they said, was invulnerability toward coercion, and that is what they sought.) They had some obvious problems with maintaining contact and have largely vanished today.

But not before they had made rudimentary attempts at solving the problem of beating the State and remaining part of society. After all, the State and human society are natural enemies; it should be possible to use society as an ally against the State. (Remember the social standing of snitches?)

They called the concept of interaction with the rest of society (those not "vonu") interfacing. This was brought up last chapter in our explanation of counter-economic banking, and that was one set of examples.

One way to interface with the rest of the economy, especially the White Market or Overground or Establishment Economy, is to create another identity. Let this fictitious individual take the risks; you can drop the identity when it appears to be near apprehension.

There are some serious problems with The Paper Trip[2] approach. To put it simply, if the State's agents are closing in on this alter-ego, as long as you wear the guise they are closing in on *you*.

Also, once you "shed the skin," you lose everything that went with it: accounts, contacts, acquaintances, and property stored under that name. It is a smaller loss than arrest and possible imprisonment, but it is no solution.

Multiple identities — if you can keep them straight — are an improvement.

The answer is not to abandon secondary identities nor to depend upon them. The technique is best used as a back-up — anti-arrest insurance. And using some sort of dummy company or identity is inescapable for counter-economic real estate.

This leads to the natural categorization of information flow into a system of layers. With each layer, there are appropriate counter-economic techniques, some long-standing and successful, others yet to be developed by bright young innovators.

Inner-Layer Information Flow

The innermost core of information about you is made up of you and your intimates. Some people need work on themselves — learning when to say what to whom. And selection of one's spouse and family on the basis of their discretion may appear a bit unromantic or biologically restrained. Fortunately, a long-standing tradition in many families of keeping sensitive information "in the family" works in one's favor here.

The next layer is that between you and your friends and distant family. Notice how inquiries about income and business practices are considered bad taste socially. Perhaps that is an indication of society's natural evolution toward agorism.

The final inner layer may be the most risky: customers, clients, suppliers, and partners who not only know something specific about you but, if you get too close to them, they are in a position to have the "second two" to put two and two together.

There are two useful techniques to control this information flow; one is to follow the useful social rule against mixing business and pleasure. This must be done carefully so as not to excite suspicion that you're hiding something — a tantalization that few can resist probing. This technique leads to putting your commercial associates in the next layer.

But there is another technique: swap risks. If you have something on them, you are far less worried about them finding out something on you. This is a form of swapping of intimacies, so, as in romantic relations, choose your associates carefully.

"You mean you're Counter-Economic, too?" may well be the most common sigh of relief in the 1990s.

Middle-Layer Information Flow

Innermost of all commercial information are your records. Who, besides you, should see your books? If all goes well, *no one* should.

Nor, with all the trust in the world, is there a good reason to give others so much access to your information flow that they are able to piece together your books like a jigsaw puzzle (e.g., forensic accounting). It is possible you may need to open your books concerning a specific venture or one of your business enterprises if you involve others in investment; this can be handled counter-economically.

Such enterprises are useful for distancing yourself from unfriendly information gatherers by adding an extra layer for their penetration.

The middle layer (a mesosphere, the scientists would call it) of information flow is the interesting part. Here is where your casual interactions with others lie.

An obvious virtue or good habit to develop is never to reveal information pertaining to your counter-economic activities, or — before you do — you consciously consider the consequences. "Talk to you tomorrow about that, Jane; I've got to check something first," gives you 24 hours of risk-weighing.

Still, if you are going to deal with the rest of the world, you must reveal some information: that you have a product or service, how much it will cost, what you will accept in payment, how you can be contacted, and when are you or it available. If there are multiple payments, credit arrangements, repeat business, and post-sale follow-up involved, still more information must flow from you.

And toward you as well. Another good technique is the information swap. As you reveal something, you learn something from your supplier or customer.

If you discover your counterpart is also counter-economic, keep the relief somewhat contained. You still need to find out how counter-economic. After all, there are counter-economic cops and even IRS agents! Everyone breaks laws some of the time; it is impossible not to.

But that works for you more than against you. For if it's not obvious that your client or tradesman is counter-economic, you have to make the step yourself to cross the line. And since everyone is somewhat counter-economic, it is not obvious that you are suggesting anything out of the ordinary except in this limited case.

This is far easier than it sounds. Hundreds of times this author has gone to printers and suggested they don't waste receipt papers and drop the sales tax. Refusal came only when the mistake was made of talking to a non-decisionmaker. Beware even the smallest bureaucracy. Cabbies in New York will offer to leave the flag up if you don't look too much like a law enforcer — and if you ask first, jump at the offer.

At least at present, North American society has pressured the government court system to frown on entrapment. It will change, but while it's in effect, it is a great boon for Counter-Economists breaking the ice.[3]

Personal contact has the advantage of allowing a counter-economic courtship rite. But there is a corresponding giveaway of information about you by allowing another's observation. It's a trade-off. As always in Counter-Economics, you must weigh the risks against the benefits in each particular situation.

Consider, then, the benefits of impersonal contact from advertisement and word of mouth, correspondence, delivery via (possibly counter-economic) couriers, and payment by mail, courier, or even through counter-economic banks. At this point, it's time to haul out the computer.

Computers for Counter-Economics

Consider the following scenario: Someone in the market for, say, custom footwear, consults a list of products. Seeing the category of footwear, she calls up a list of suppliers. One of them happens to offer fancy work and gives an access code. The code is activated.

A list of offerings appears. She requests something not quite on this list, say, a pair of high deerskin boots with elvish runes stitched in, suitable for a fantasy convention or Society for Creative Anachronism gathering. A sketch appears of such boots, with specification numbers and costs, depending on type of trim.

The order is placed and a deposit agreed upon. The deposit is transferred via the countereconomic bank (or maybe to a mail drop). The boots are delivered, found satisfactory, and the balance paid. Neither party to the transaction has revealed herself to the other.

Anyone familiar with today's computer technology knows that not only is all this feasible but already exists, in whole or in part, in most major cities and university towns.

Imagine further that you can keep your records in books under a complicated code that would require more trouble than you're worth to crack. And that you can advertise on the computer bulletin board with similar codes and contact and be contacted through such codes.

Again, the technology is available, or, as the hackers say, "on line" It's a dream come true for Counter-Economists: a nightmare in the making for the IRS and the government's regulators and controllers.

The "key" is Public Key Cryptography. The National Security Agency (NSA, colloquially known as "The Puzzle Palace") hates it and is working on cracking the systems and getting businesses and bureaucracies to agree to a standardized system they can easily crack. It should be kept in mind that cryptography is a dynamic, evolving system. It is a non-violent form of an arms race where one side cracks the code and the other develops a new system to top the old one. Those considering using this should check the current literature and talk with computer-hip friends. (The usual problem is to keep them on a narrow subject.) A popular source, available in most libraries, to keep you current in public-key cryptography is *Byte* magazine.

You and your correspondent(s) define a *cryptosystem*. The sender has an *encryption* key; the recipient has a *decryption* key. They are not identical. The normal message may be called *plaintext* and the encrypted form *ciphertext*.

"Cryptographic keys are analogous to the house and car keys we carry in our daily lives and serve a similar purpose. In many modern systems, each key is a string of digits. For example, keys defined by the Data Encryption Standard of the National Bureau of Standards consist of 64 binary digits, 56 of which are significant."[4]

How does it work? "To encrypt a message, a key and the message are somehow inserted into an encryptor, and the cryptogram that emerges is a jumble of characters that depends on both the message and the key. To decrypt the message, the correct key and the cryptogram are inserted into a decryptor, and the plaintext message emerges."[5]

This is quite simple with conventional coding. The keys are the same, must be closely guarded, and you must visit your correspondent to exchange keys. But using public keys, the problem of meeting and secrecy is solved.

"These keys… have remarkable, almost magical properties:

• for each encryption key there is a decryption key, which is not the same as the encryption key
• it is feasible to compute a pair of keys, consisting of an encryption key and a corresponding decryption key
• it is not feasible to compute the decryption key from knowledge of the encryption key."[6]

You and your correspondent, say, Mary, can counter-economically contact each other on a "public" bulletin board. Agreeing to exchange information, you set up your encryption. "To set it up, you generate a pair of keys, and send the encryption key to Mary by any convenient means. It need not be kept secret. It can only encrypt messages — not decrypt them. Revealing it discloses nothing useful about the decryption key.... To allow you to send private messages to her, Mary must similarly create a pair of keys and send her encryption key to her."[7]

You may publicize your encryption key with no fear that anyone but you can decrypt the message. "Any two people with directory entries could then communicate privately, even if they had no previous contact."[8] Exactly what counter-economists want.

A Touch of Tech and a Knapsack

Before leaving this subject, let us touch briefly on the technology. One may look up the programming in the cited source and, in a world of adventurous hackers, no one should find great difficulty in getting a programmer to set up whatever one needs on one's home system.

What one requires from Information pyrotechnics and arcane-seeming codes is a reasonable confidence and qualified respect. Unfortunately, many whom I have witnessed coming across this field bounce from awe and feeling that the State is defeated to depression and resignation when they hear a particular system has been cracked. Let us try to immunize you against both.

The awe arises from statistics like the one published about the Rivest-Shamir-Adleman (RSA) cryptosystem. The amount of time required to crack the code is the factoring time; assuming your key length is 50, it could be factored in 3.9 hours at one computer operation per microsecond. But doubling the key length to 100 digits kicks up the factoring time to 74 years and tripling it to 150 digits makes it one million years to factor! By the time we get to 250 digits, we're exceeding the estimated lifespan of the universe. Small wonder NSA wants to standardize key length at 60 to 70 digits.

A 77-digit key was recently available for $165 for the common z80 system. "...message encryption and decryption take about one minute plus the necessary disk access time. The time needed to generate the encryption and decryption keys ranges from 15 minutes to 4 hours.... The author of the system, Charles Merritt of PKS, Inc., has received estimates of the time needed to break the system ranging from three uninterrupted days on a Cray-1 to one year."[9]

In fact, newer and faster computers than the Cray-1 are up or on the way, but one can easily outpace them by increasing the number of digits in the RSA key. Still, one should be aware of the state of the art when playing this game.

An alternate to the RSA, the Knapsack Scheme, seemed preferable because of faster encryption and decryption. The name comes from a mathematical puzzle where if one knows the total weight of a knapsack and its contents, and the weights of the individual items that may be in the knapsack, one deduces which items are packed inside. For a numerical code, the items are a collection of numbers and the knapsack is their sum.

Martin Hellman of Stanford University and Ralph C. Merkle used the technique to devise a public-key cryptosystem in 1978. Merkle offered a reward for anyone who could break the scheme and the game was afoot.

"In 1982, Shamir made the first successful attack in the simplest form of the knapsack cryptosystem. He found that certain information about superincreasing sequences is not well disguised by a modular multiplication trapdoor. In addition, that information could be secured rapidly by solving a special kind of mathematics problem (finding a short vector in a lattice). Shamir's method became practical with the invention of an algorithm for solving this problem quickly. Soon after, using a similar approach, Adleman broke another form of the knapsack cryptosystems known as the Graham-Shamir knapsack."[10]

Shamir collected the $100 prize but Merkle offered another $1000 to anyone breaking the more complex iterated knapsack. Ernest F. Brickell of the Sandia National Laboratories in Albuquerque, New Mexico, went after the prize in the summer of 1984. In October, "Merkle conceded that Brickell had won the prize and Brickell received his check.... Says Merkle 'I think the breaking of iterated knapsacks is quite surprising and indicates a degree of insecurity that had not been suspected at all.'"[11]

Is it time for information counter-economists to panic? No, and this is why they need to maintain awareness of the fast-changing field: "However, this doesn't rule out the possibility that a secure knapsack cryptosystem exists. Brickell adds,

'What this says is that if you use one, you have to use something other than modular arithmetic for hiding it.' ... Of course, cryptologists can't resist the challenge of coming up with a cryptosystem that circumvents the flaws pinpointed by Brickell's decryption technique. At Crypto '84, Rivest and Benny Cho were ready with a new knapsack public-key cryptosystem based on arithmetic in mathematical structures called 'finite fields.'"[12]

While computer cryptographers play the game of better mouse vs. better mousetrap, Adi Shamir raises the stakes and offers hope that a counter-economically invulnerable (within reason) cryptosystem may be developed — or at least the cost of it can be rationally calculated.

"'The most intriguing question is whether you can develop proof techniques that will show the security of cryptosystems,' says Shamir. 'If you could do this, it would be the biggest breakthrough in cryptography because at last you would be able to show that concrete cryptosystems just will not be broken in the future unless there is a certain amount of time.'"[13]

As in all Counter-Economics, the risks need to be rationally calculated and the pay-off traded off against the potential profit. With computers and counter-economic programs, this can be accomplished simpler, easier, and faster than ever. Add to this the potential of inexpensive high security of records and message exchange, and one need not ask for miraculous invulnerability to the State's authorized robbers.

But something like that miracle may be provided by the market anyway, and fairly soon. Having moved information successfully in the Counter-Economy, the next trick is to move physical objects as safely and efficiently. Fortunately, as we see in the next chapter, the market has a very long history in successful shipping Counter-Economics, that is, Smuggling.

Footnotes

1. But not entirely. In December 1984 the National Security Agency announced plans to develop a new-generation system, with greater speed and capacity than

existing ones. See the later section on Public Key Cryptography for the prime reason why.

2. Reid, B. (1971). The Paper Trip. Fountain Valley, California: Eden Press. (A well-known counter-economic text, with updates such as The Paper Trip II, 1977, The Paper Trip III, 1998, and [now with non-Roman numerals] The Paper Trip 4, 2015.)

3. An irresistible aside. Americans have a clear-cut double standard on entrapment which is joy to the Counter-Economist. Entrapping businessmen — even big businessmen like John DeLorean — is a no-no; yet entrapping politicians (arch-statists), such as those caught in FBI's Abscam, is proper. The difference is this: the politicians have no legitimate business with any special interest group; or, to put it more strongly but still in the American tradition, "all politicians are crooks" and assumed to be (potentially, at least) up to no good.

4. Smith, J. (1983, January). Public key cryptography. Byte 8(1), p. 198.

5. Ibid., p. 199.

6. Ibid., p. 200.

7. Ibid.

8. Rivest, R. L., Shamir, A., & Adleman, L. (1978). A method for obtaining digital signatures and public-key cryptosystems. Communications of the Association for Computing Machinery 21(2), pp. 120-126. doi 10.1145/359340.359342.

9. Smith, op. cit., p. 216 (Editor's Note).

10. Peterson, I. (1984, November 24). The unpacking of a knapsack. Science News 126(21), p. 331.

11. Ibid.

12. Ibid.

13. Ibid.

Chapters Seven through Ten

These chapters are rumored to exist in digital format somewhere in the cyberverse. When they are located, they will be added to an updated version of Counter-Economics. The remainder of Counter-Economics — Chapters Eleven through Eighteen — was not completed before SEK3's untimely death. He left an outline of all the chapters, which is included to demonstrate the breadth, depth, and social import of the science of Counter-Economics.

Outline
(These are Konkin's personal notes describing his vision for *Counter-Economics*)

Part One
Preface (Optional)
To be written by "name" writer or writers such as Doug Casey, Harry Browne, Mur ray Rothbard, Thomas Szasz, Karl Hess, John Pugsley, and so on.

Introduction
Written. Summarizes complexity of the theme of the book in simple terms. Promises enjoyable survey of this strange, new field with economic theory in a back section and ideological explanation at the very end. Up-front about intention but soft- sell and low-key in presentation.

Chapter One: Tax Counter-Economics
Written. Very detailed survey of the American "underground economy," the taxless part of the whole Counter-Economy. All examples are taken from well-known, "Establishment" news sources. Critics of mass tax evasion quoted and they are very sketchily answered, to tantalize the readers for later theory.

Chapter Two: International Counter-Economics
Written. First third or so of this chapter hops around the globe, Western Europe, and the "Third World," with a tax Counter-Economics approach. Second third covers transitionally Marxist-Leninist Third World countries and corresponding in- crease in counter-economic activity. The final third moves into the "Eastern bloc" and follows increasing shift of total market to black, underground, or left-hand. Zero in on the U.S.S.R. do we as the last hope for the State to crush the Counter- Economy.

Chapter Three: Soviet Counter-Economics
Written. This chapter is closest to a single view of the scope and depth possible in a society that has gone almost completely Counter-Economic. The helplessness of the Soviet State is stressed and shown by repeated examples. The possibilities of Counter Economics beyond narrow fields of business are introduced to whet the reader's appetite for the rest of the book. Russian

millionaires are exhibited to prove points.

Chapter Four: Drug Counter-Economics

Written. This chapter is obligatory as "Drug Connections" and the corresponding network are the most popular view and popular understanding of black-market activities. Therefore, readers' expectations will be played against. First, the size and scope of the market, up to taking over governments when convenient, is shown. Second, a brief sketch of how the market works from producer to dealer. *Twist*: the latter part of this chapter will use the drug market to show the *interconnectedness* of nearly everyone in society, complicity of casual customers, friends, colleagues, relatives, even passersby — a social conspiracy against the government. This is then compared to the Prohibition Era for historical continuity and to Laetrile-dealing to show its expansion outside "vice" drugs. "What's a drug?": who says and why. The drug *business* is treated as a counter-economic paradigm, with similarities and differences to "regular" business.

Chapter Five: Inflation Counter-Economics

Written. Begins with heavy reference to existent doom-and-gloom writers such as Browne, Casey, Schulz, Pugsley, etc. The Survivalist Movement is tied in with inflation and its Counter-Economics. Some theory snuck in here to explain inflation and contrast it with rising-price phenomenon. The Austrian business cycle is sketched to give a basis for doom 'n' gloom. Gold gets a special section, both legally and illegally owned and traded, and other precious metals, commodities, "Alpha Strategy" purchases, right down to retreats and stashes. The historical gold standard, its return (possibly) and State's fear of it will lead to the next section. The final section deals with some innovations in the grey market such as 100%-gold banking offered by underground "banker" and detailed description of his activities. The value of counter-economists trading with other counter-economists is explained here. Modern computers make barter accounting and underground resource transfer feasible on larger and larger scale.

Chapter Six: Information Counter-Economics

Written. Rapid rise of computer industry, individualistic nature of freelance consulting, computer privateers and pirates are chronicled. Government has thrown up its hands at regulation of this industry. Discussion is then divided into two types of counter-economic computer and information activities.

Counter-Economics for Information Industry
Wheeling and dealing, under-the-table trading, and various dodges by counter-economists from researchers and consultants to keypunchers and programmers to owners and franchisers, will be covered. Mass-media examples will be given for convincing the readers.

Information Industry for Counter-Economics
Data encryption and new techniques of libertarian examples. Carl Nikolai is introduced with his original work in this field. The applications of state-proof data processing for tax evasion, inflation-evasion, dealing and other sorts of marketeering are shown, both those already working and those which are immediate possibilities.

The Lost Chapters

Chapter Seven: Smuggling Counter-Economics
Biggest smugglers may come as a surprise to the readers: nearly everyone at Customs check-ins; this will open the chapter for reader identification. Statistics will be given, brightly and spritely as usual.

Money & Currency Smuggling
This section begins with references to previous six chapters worked in here; they will remind readers of what they have learned (in a subtle way). Currency control ties into tax evasion, drug dealing, and the Red (Communist) black markets, and even information processing.

Historical Smuggling
This will be a historical tour and brief description of the classic, stereotypical concept of smuggling and its modern hangover is dealt with, mostly to dispense with it and contrast it to…

Border-Crossing For Profit
This will deal with how most international companies move goods across borders (or say they do) to beat taxes, tariffs, Value Added Taxes, Sales Taxes, import quotas, and so on (also done by small businesses and individuals). Crossing state

lines to avoid sales tax and other controls is also covered here. This section ties in nearly all businesses of every size to the Counter-Economy.

Contraband Counter-Economics
What is and isn't legal varies widely from State to State (and state to state and province to province and county to county and…). The concept of entrepreneurship is explored here using "moving goods from low-price to high-price areas" as starting point for the idea. This is a subtle introduction of some real economics.

Rhodesian Paper Chase
How the oil embargo of Rhodesia was beaten by Mobil Oil: multinational industry smuggling will be spelled out in adventurous detail. Example illustrates large-scale
end of counter-economic operations, acceptability among the "higher circles" of finance, and its potential to shake governments.

What Isn't Smuggling?
Trade in violation of regulation could even cover deals between neighbors, carrying favors for friends, even private mail delivery. This section emphasizes universality of smuggling. Smuggling Bibles and religious material is mentioned. Smuggling "people" is introduced, to be used in the "Human Counter-Economics" Chapter, with underground railway of the Civil War period. Tie-in to information industry (Chapter Six) and transportation problems (Chapter Eight).

Chapter Eight: Transportation Counter-Economics
The need to move things is basic. Methods will be listed: foot, private vehicles, commercial transportation, and government-controlled public means; example of counter-economic use of all will be given.

Citizen's Band Counter-Economics
This wild section will tell how CB beats traffic laws and increases profit for truckers. Actual (simple) economic calculations will be made. Statistics will be given on the size of the market. Why is agricultural trucking exempt from most trucking regulation and how is that used? Lurid examples of counter-economic

trucking and how it was romanticized by C&W music, movies and TV, and radio. Is this a model for spreading other forms and kinds of Counter-Economics? The rise of British CB use, completely illegal, is covered.

Moving People Counter-Economically

New York Gypsy cabs triumph over the regulators. Also covered will be jitneys; "Grey Rabbit" buses; private car-pools that evolve into underground busing and taxiing; "hippie" airlines — why it took off and why it failed; and even hitchhiking.

Ocean Counter-Economics

Small boat owners beat controls in various examples. Potential and actual usage of boats for counter-economic purposes are also covered, such as barges of marijuana along the Florida coast. Smuggling is tied in, of course. A bit of futurism will be added with a discussion of the Sea-Bed Treaty and counter-economic implications for Ocean-Bed mining, ranching in the seas, and even ocean habitats.

Air Counter-Economics

Freddie Laker takes on regulations and the recent airline deregulations as examples of responses to airlines' "bending" the rules — Counter-Economics! There will be examples of plane use for drug smuggling, diamond smuggling, courier activity, nearly everything on both private planes and commercial air traffic.

Space Counter-Economics

OTRAG will kick off this chapter, the private space industry both aboveground and underground; movement in various popular space groups *away* from NASA and government monopoly of space. Both actual and speculative cases will be surveyed.

Chapter Nine: Energy Counter-Economics

First, energy sources will be surveyed as to counter-economic and establishment use: tapping public lines, faking stocks, private sources kept and exploited. Survivalists and ecologists are moving together out of regulated power grid for con- verging reasons. Both high-tech and low-tech alternatives to the market will be covered. The sham of government "incentives" for small-scale energy alternatives and solar will be exposed as actually protecting monopolistic power companies. This will lead into an explanation of history of government regulation and its causation of nearly all current pollution and energy waste. Some speculation will be added at the end to indicate how a powerful counter-economy (and weak state) would handle pollution and conservation. This will tie-in with the Justice Counter-Economics chapter.

Chapter Ten: Human Counter-Economics

This chapter should eliminate any lingering doubts about Counter-Economics being cold and heartless. Sections will cover **Illegal Aliens**, especially Mexican border, but also Asiatics, Canadians, Australians, and Europeans; labor as a counter- economic good; **Underground Railway** slaves moved counter-economically, variants of it still in use; **Refugees** covers Counter-Economics of freeing people from greater tyranny but should they even bother leaving their existing Counter- Economy? What *is* a free country (a little more theory snuck in here)? Minority groups are covered here first, how they survive in hostile societies, and the sub- societies they form, usually overwhelmingly counter-economic — a hint of possible communities for hard-core counter-economists will be introduced here but developed near the end of the book.

The Unwritten Chapters

Chapter Eleven: Dissenters and Intellectual Counter- Economics

This chapter should grab the academics and the more intellectual critics. Under-ground political, religious, and academic activity and the marketing of that dissent in North America, South America, Europe, the Third World, and, of course, Eastern Europe, will be exemplified. Underground newspapers and underground publishing. A separate section may be developed on education alternatives, the difference between public schools, private schools, and independent schools and then out-and-out underground schools will be detailed. A little more theory can be safely spelled out here.

Chapter Twelve: Sex Counter-Economics

"Everybody's doing it" will be the theme here, with statistics on violation of sex laws; lists of those laws in various states and countries, and various attitudes will be given, too — nearly everything is illegal and nearly no one cares.

Pornography
Definitions vary and these will be noted. Business methods of dealing with local codes will be spelled out. Classified advertising in street-sold sex newspapers in Southern California will be cited and exhibited as a model for other types of counter-economic business transaction and advertising needs.

Prostitution
"World's oldest profession" is counter-economic: women, men, adolescents — everyone — and it's admitted by authorities to be unstoppable everywhere. Amusing anecdotes about bondage- and dominance-fantasizing politicians will be told for spice and to make a point. Where does one draw the line between cohabitation and prostitution will be asked and answered. Morality and ethics of the business will be discussed but it will lead into following chapters: Psychological self-awareness and freedom of expression leads directly to the next two chapters.

Chapter Thirteen: Feminist Counter-Economics
This will begin with a review of the sex laws of the previous chapters but with a slant on sexual discrimination and how counter-economic activity gets around the State.

Home Birth Counter-Economics
The Home Birth Movement, largely illegal in the 1980s, is covered in some detail — the Midwife as Counter-Economist. History of smuggling and contraband of birth control information fits in here.

Equality of Counter-Economic Opportunity
This can be considered general for all minority groups, but women are the largest and thus will be focused on: how the Counter-Economy is sex-blind, color-blind, and creed-blind; the segment further develops the theme of sub-societies embedded in society-at-large. Aspect which will be developed is how minorities use the Counter-Economy to break out of ghettos, barrios, and menial employment in North America and abroad. Gays will be covered here and in

Chapter Twelve. The futility of the ERA and such laws will be shown and give an opportunity for a little theoretical explanation.

Chapter Fourteen: Justice Counter-Economics

This chapter will, in some senses, tie in with nearly all the other chapters because it will answer the burning question in the readers' minds: how can justice and contracts be maintained without government; in fact, with government as an active enemy of both contract and justice?

Failure of Government Justice

Why the government cannot deliver protection or justice leads off this section. Lots of examples, mostly in modern-day America, will be cited. The "climate of fear" and the perennial "crime problem" of "law and order" as a political football will be exploded.

Protection Business

Why catching criminals is too late for most people's good, though the Counter-Economy will even provide that service. The technology of protection and defence will be handled in great detail right up to the latest devices and their market popularity, and even ones yet to be introduced, right up to science-fiction possibilities.

Natural Law and Its Enforcement

The concept of Natural Law is introduced. The spontaneous order of the market will be explained, heavily illustrated both in "straight" transactions and counter-economic dealings. The stigma of "finking" as a more general concept and is validity will be developed. Finally, the reader will be given counter-economic law enforcement and criminal apprehension procedures. The "protection racket" is explicitly excluded but "loan sharking" will be dealt with as more complex and deserving of some sympathy.

Arbitration and Counter-Economics

Arbitration is already big in the aboveground and cases like the Johnny Carson-NBC contract dispute resolution will be cited, as well as statistics from the American Arbitration Association. Beginning of a Libertarian Arbitration

Association will be delineated, and tying it in with "blacklists" and "white lists" will develop a working concept of Counter-Economic Justice.

Chapter Fifteen: Psychology Counter-Economics
The theme of this chapter is the reinforcement of psychological "good health", that is, self-reliance and taking responsibility, with objective *actions* — which turn out to be counter-economic.

Authoritarianism
Research on this subject, especially as compiled by Dr. Sharon Presley, will be presented showing the links between obedience-conditioning and statism.

Human Potential Movement All the various aspects of the New Psychology will be shown compatible with counter-economic activity, and even congruent. Not only Presley, Thomas Szasz, and Nathaniel Branden, but even psychologists not identified with libertarianism will be cited.

How It Works
Concrete cases, anonymous, of course, will be summarized here for illustrating counter-economic psychology.

Mutual Reinforcement
Going beyond individual self-reliance and self-acceptance, the concept of individuals working together counter-economically, developing trust and honest in- terdependence, will finally be developed (after popping up briefly all over the book). Beyond relationships and affinity groups, we come logically to the idea of an active sub-society and/or Movement of Counter-Economists — and that brings us to Part II.

Part Two
Chapter Sixteen: Understanding Counter-Economics
"Why am I so smart?" theme kicks off this chapter. "How come the author understands all this when the rest of society has 'caught on' only in part, at best?" will tease the reader into finally diving into the theory. Answers: (1) There is a well-worked, proven theory that has done wonders in predicting human action and describing it in a scientific manner (this chapter) and (2) There is a strong

vested interest — the strongest in all history — to confuse the issue and distort your information to save its privileges (next chapter). The value of understanding economics to immunize one from "con games" will be stressed to pull the reader along.

Praxeology: The Study of Human Action
Fairly simple (non-academic) but still rigorous presentation of basic concepts of Austrian Economics such as subjective value, marginal utility, time preference (originary rate of interest), regression (money's origin), the capital pyramid of Eugen Böhm-Bawerk and the business cycle of Ludwig Von Mises. Both everyday examples for reader identification and counter-economic examples will be used to maintain reader interest.

Why Counter-Economics Works
Kicking off with the distinction of profit from "rate of return," entrepreneurship is reintroduced and then applied to all aspects of daily life. (This ties in with the previous chapter — selfreliance, but now acceptance of risk is stressed.) The key to understanding and practicing Counter-Economics is now spelled out: trade risk for profit. The whole experience of the book is linked to back this.

How Counter-Economics Works
A formula will be given, simple algebra, which can be used for day-to-day business calculations, using readily available data, to calculate risk taken to see if it is acceptable — maximum estimated risk, at that! A few caveats about embarking on a counter-economic lifestyle and disclaimers that the author is "advocating lawbreaking" closes out this chapter.

Chapter Seventeen: Opposing Counter-Economics
The second answer to why Counter-Economics has not yet become *the* Economics is finally given here. The nature of the opposition will be spelled out.

The Origin and Nature of The State
History and sociology of the State will be sketched out here, quickly bringing the reader to the present time with increased awareness.

Establishment Economics Ruling classes — the king and his court intellectuals

— are explained to show why the science of economics is constantly bent into fraud and con games by political "necessity." The popular myths of the day will be listed with brief descriptions.

Dead Ends
Conservativism, liberalism, socialism, anarchism, varieties of libertarianism, pacifism, "dropping out" and retreatism will all be trotted out, defined, sketched, and refuted as means of achieving a free society — again, drawing heavily on the reader's experience of the rest of the book to keep it short and sweet — or quick and deadly. Once all the other options are eliminated, that will leave the final chapter:

Chapter Eighteen: Social Counter-Economics
The promised final chapter spelling out the full integration of libertarian theory and counter-economic practice is presented. This section will eventually be expanded to a full volume with a heavier, academic style and the book will be promised to readers for a follow-up (a sort of *Counter-Economics II* for sequel lovers). The book will end with a veiled — to cover liabilities — exhortation to *live* one's theories and fulfill one's dreams. We *could* close with a description of the author's ten years in the Counter-Economy to show he practiced everything he preached (or leave it to a back-panel biography).

Bibliography & Index
Recommended reading for further interest in the various topics. An index is probably a good idea but would double the time on finishing the book. The Table of Contents could list sub-topics instead.

NOTE TO PUBLISHERS: The fact that this subject touches almost every field, and hence will be in demand as a reference in History, Sociology, Economics, Feminism, Eastern Studies, Russian Studies, Psychology, and Political Science, and is to date the *only* such work available, is not accidental but inherent in the nature of the subject. Thus, it has the rare quality of being both popular and academic in appeal... and with a little luck, so will the sequel. — SEK3

About Samuel Edward Konkin III

Samuel Edward Konkin III was a vanguard movement theorist and hard-core activist since the historic split between libertarians and conservatives at the YAF convention in St. Louis, 1969. In the subsequent three and a half decades, he served as editor and publisher of the longest-lived libertarian publication, beginning as *Lais- sez-Faire!* (1970), then as *New Libertarian Notes* (1971-75), *New Libertarian Weekly* (1975-77, the longest-running libertarian weekly), and *New Libertarian* (1978-1990). He wrote the seminal work on agorism, *New Libertarian Manifesto,* in 1980. He has coined the following terms and concepts, many of which have turned up in all libertarian publications: Counter-Economics, agorism, minarchy, partyarchy, anti-principles, Left Libertarianism, anarchozionism, "Browne-out," red market, Kochtopus, and more. He has influenced the works of authors such as J. Neil Schulman (*Alongside Night*) and Victor Koman (*Kings of the High Frontier*), who both had their first professional fiction sales in the pages of his publications. Mr. Konkin served as Executive Director of the Agorist Institute, an outreach organization promulgating the principles of agorism and counter-economics. He was a guest of honor at science-fiction conventions and libertarian gatherings and was a seasoned world traveler. *Counter-Economics* was intended to be his magnum opus, the distillation of all his work and research over 15 years of movement activism. Sadly, of the 18 chapters outlined, only ten chapters were written. Of those, only six were available at the time of publication. Mr. Konkin died February 23, 2004.

About Derrick Broze

Derrick Broze is an author, journalist, documentary filmmaker, and activist based in Houston, Texas. In 2010, Derrick founded the activist alliance The Houston Free Thinkers, organizing protests, music festivals, community gardens, skill-shares, and other community events. In 2011, he began broadcasting his radio show Free Thinker Radio, which continues to air on 90.1 KPFT in Houston. In 2013, he founded The Conscious Resistance Network, a site dedicated to multimedia journalism that exposes corporate and governmental corruption while highlighting solutions. Derrick has been producing videos, essays, and articles since 2011. In 2015, he began writing books and has released one every year since. He co-authored The Conscious Resistance trilogy with John Vibes and authored The Holistic Self-Assessment. Derrick started writing and producing documentaries in 2015. Since 2013, he has spoken in the United States, Europe, and Central America. His goal is to create a conscious agora of free humans who desire to be free of force, coercion, and violence.

Lightning Source UK Ltd.
Milton Keynes UK
UKHW010633050221
378309UK00001B/90